The Life & Times of the World's Largest Eskimo

By
Big Bob Aiken
and Lew Freedman

First Printing, 1999
Published by Glacier Press, Anchorage, Alaska
Printed by A.T. Publishing& Printing, Inc., Anchorage, Alaska

Books by Lew Freedman

Dangerous Steps: Vernon Tejas and the Solo Winter Ascent of Mount McKinley

Real Alaskans

Live from the Kenai River: Reelin' Em In with Celebrity Fishing Guide Harry Gaines

Iditarod Classics
George Attla: The Legend of the Sled Dog Trail
Live from the Tundra! Lew Freedman's Greatest Hits

Hunting the Wild Country: 40 Years As A Guide in Alaska and Wyoming (with Kenny Sailors)

Iditarod Dreams: A Year in the Life of Alaskan Sled Dog Racer DeeDee Jonrowe

Wild Times in Wild Places, Adventures on Alaska's Frontier

Iditarod Silver

Fishing For A Laugh

Dedication

I would like to dedicate this book to my parents, Robert and Martha Aiken. Thanks to them for the gift of life they and God gave me and the gift of love I received from them in my upbringing.
—— Big Bob Aiken

Table of Contents

Introduction 1
Chapter 1 7
Chapter 2 11
Chapter 3 19
Chapter 4 23
Chapter 5 29
Chapter 6 33
Chapter 7 39
Chapter 8 49
Chapter 9 55
Chapter 10 59
Chapter 11 67
Chapter 12 71
Chapter 13 75
Photographs 81
Chapter 14 89
Chapter 15 95
Chapter 16 101
Chapter 17 107
Chapter 18 115
Chapter 19 119
Chapter 20 123
Chapter 21 129
Chapter 22 135
Chapter 23 139
Chapter 24 143
Chapter 25 147
Chapter 26 153
Chapter 27 157
Chapter 28 161
Chapter 29 167
Chapter 30 171

Introduction

Strength and wisdom. Those words sum up my first impression of Big Bob Aiken.

In July of 1987, I attended the World Eskimo-Indian Olympics at the Big Dipper Ice Arena in Fairbanks for the first time. The annual four-day festival celebrates with dance and sporting events a subsistence way of life once common throughout the world.

Big Bob (everyone calls him that) was a competitor. He was nearing the end of his long reign as the king of the Games' strength events, the dominant figure in events such as the four-man carry, the arm pull, and the Eskimo and Indian stick pulls.

I watched him win the Eskimo stick pull with a simple shrug of power. And I saw him win the Indian stick pull by holding tight with his thick fingers and easily yanking the implement away from all challengers. I also listened to him talk, telling stories about the origins of the unique games of the north, how Native villagers who rely on a subsistence hunting and fishing lifestyle invented the competitions.

Over time I came to understand the rules of these and other sports so foreign to the average American sports fan, as well as their history and meaning. Big Bob was a gracious teacher and through his explanations I came to understand how Eskimo play reflected the hard life in the far north which revolved around fishing, hunting, whaling and withstanding harsh winter elements.

Big Bob has a commanding presence in many ways. As self-proclaimed and undisputed World's Largest Eskimo he stands six-feet-four and weighs three-hundred-and-thirty pounds. The phrase about a man needing no introduction was invented for Big Bob. Anyone walking into a crowded room can easily identify him, even if they have never met him. Big Bob towers over the scene.

Size alone is only one reason why a meeting with Big Bob is unforgettable. He is a soft-spoken man whose voice is a low rumble. He has a wry sense of humor and laughs often. Above all, however, he is a passionate spokesman for the Native way of life, a stirring defender of the old ways of a culture squeezed by the encroachment of western civilization in a modern Alaska that is rapidly changing.

"He's a continuum," said Brian Randazzo, a World Eskimo-Indian Olympics competitor from Anchorage who is one of the greatest Native sports athletes and is one of Big Bob's close friends. "He's going to be an excellent elder because tiny kids to adults identify with Big Bob. He's a communications link."

Big Bob's life itself is a link, straddling the transformation of his home, Barrow, Alaska over the last four decades. He is both old enough to have lived an old-style way and young enough to have adjusted to a new way.

Once, Big Bob and his family chopped up the ice of the Arctic Ocean for their water. Now they obtain their drinking water from a faucet. Once, Big Bob and his family traveled across the flat, snowy northern plains by dog sled, then snowmachine. Now he owns a Chevy Suburban. Once, Big Bob and his family ate only the fish and game meat they captured or killed themselves. Now there is a modern grocery store in the heart of Barrow. What a special treat it is now to be able to buy lettuce on a daily basis, instead of having it be a rare treat when a visiting friend steps off the plane carrying it as a gift purchased at a store in a distant city.

A modern man and an ancient man all at once, that is Big Bob. He will snack on a candy bar, but would be a disgruntled fellow indeed if he could not also devour some sweet muktuk, the meat from a bowhead whale. He works a regular day job operating heavy machinery for the North Slope Borough, a huge area encompassing much of the northern section of Alaska, but he also hunts for bearded seal and whale in skinboats.

Although he is only in his mid-forties, Big Bob gently dispenses information to youngsters in the manner of a wise elder. They look up to him and listen carefully when the words of other adult authority figures might evaporate into thin air. The littlest of children gravitates to Big Bob, squeezing his legs with friendly hugs, showering him with affection.

This aspect of Big Bob signifies the man he has become during a life's journey. Once Big Bob himself would have ignored the advice and wisdom offered by someone like Big Bob. Now a much-admired adult citizen, Big Bob struggled dramatically with his own growing pains as a youth. Now a spokesman for sobriety, like many of his Eskimo people, he struggled to overcome alcoholism. The same man who was a high school dropout has educated himself by absorbing and experiencing life.

Much of who Big Bob is reflects his environment. An Inupiat Eskimo whose people populated the cold, northern regions of Alaska thousands of years ago, and learned to fight the wintry elements to a standstill, Big Bob is a child of rural Barrow, an adult of modern Barrow.

Barrow itself is the northernmost settlement in the United States, a surprisingly bustling city of more than 4,000 people, some sixty percent of whom are Inupiat. In the other states a community of 4,000 is usually a drive-through speck on the map. Barrow is a regional hub for numerous far north Eskimo villages.

Barrow is located eight hundred miles north of Anchorage, Alaska's principal city. It is also three hundred miles north of the Arctic Circle, on flat, treeless, tundra, and well north of the forbidding Alaska Brooks Range, the mountains which cut a swath through the rugged countryside where few people dwell.

To most people who have never visited the community, Barrow is likely still most familiar for an event which occurred more than sixty years ago, a tragedy which focused the eyes of the world on the remote north for months. In August 1935, a plane piloted by famed aviator Wiley Post, and carrying beloved writer and entertainer Will Rogers as its only passenger, crashed twelve miles from town, killing both men.

A memorial was ultimately erected to the men and is located only a few blocks from Big Bob's home. Barrow attracts some eight thousand tourists a year — the vast majority in the summer — and a main attraction is the stone monument commemorating the lives and deaths of Post and Rogers. Those who come to study the site of this familiar incident, leave enriched with knowledge gained of local culture.

As a youth, Big Bob lived much the same life as his ancestors did, adjusting to the rhythms of the extreme seasons, relying on the bounty of the land to fill the dinner table. Inupiat children learn early to respect the harsh environment, to never take for granted either the difficult terrain or the powerful winds that blow in from the sea. Barrow is a community at the mercy of winters of such severity that it is not uncommon to see temperatures in the twenties and snow falling in late June. In the winter the thermometer might record temperatures of fifty degrees below zero.

Life in Barrow is also defined by another dramatic extreme unfamiliar to most of the rest of the planet. It is so far north that it features twenty-four hours of daylight in the summer and twenty-four hours of darkness in winter. Light and dark. Symbols of the seasons. The light often represents lightness of heart, playfulness under the Midnight Sun, when clocks are ignored. The darkness represents the struggle against the elements at their most brutal, when time creeps by.

After my first encounter with Big Bob in Fairbanks, we met many times at the World Eskimo-Indian Olympics and elsewhere. A friendship developed.

I visited Barrow in the winter, once when the sun never rose above the horizon, leaving the city shrouded in a dim half-light. I was surprised simply because it wasn't pitch black all the time. Another time, I witnessed the sun rising after its slumber for the first time in the new year. A narrow band of orange glowed in the distant sky for about an hour.

Everywhere I looked on these winter trips signs were posted warning the careless hiker against walkabouts in the dark because of the threat posed by polar bears. For those who grow cautious upon viewing "Beware of Dog" signs, that is indeed a vivid reminder that Barrow is not a place to be taken lightly, that a stroll there is not an everyday walk in the park.

Polar bears do come into town, and the most dangerous of these carnivores do attack human beings. The huge white beasts have no fear of man and they are very efficient hunters.

I had never seen a polar bear in the wild and prevailed upon Big Bob to drive me to the outskirts of town where the animals might roam in the dark. We took the ride, but I saw no bears. We were safe in a sturdy vehicle, but we were not close enough. However, two days after I left town, a polar bear wandered into the heart of the community along the path I covered on foot between the high school and city hall. It was shot dead.

Barrow is not the place for the vacationer seeking bright lights or Broadway-quality theatre. Although its inhabitants are Americans, it's probably best to consider Barrow as a friendly foreign outpost. The custom and culture is so different from mainstream America. Many residents speak Inupiaq as a first language — Big Bob is one — and learn English as a second language. People hunt not for trophies, but for food. There are no bars and nowhere in town is alcohol legally sold, though individuals may bring it to town for personal use. Several close votes in the early 1990s produced that controversial result.

During a week-long summer visit to Barrow, I lived in the two-story, modern home of Big Bob and his parents, Robert and Martha Aiken. I watched Robert create handmade ulu knives, the carving tools used by his people for centuries. The knives have wooden handles and half-moon shaped blades, and Robert sharpened them with patience. Finally, he set aside a finished knife, smiled, and said softly, "I think that could cut something."

Sure enough, during my June stay it snowed a few times. Perhaps just to emphasize the point of Barrow's cantankerous wintry ties. Once the thick flakes blew hard and horizontal across a restaurant picture window, creating the illusion that we were all existing in a paperweight. In a week the temperature rarely touched forty degrees.

Only a few days earlier, though, it had soared to an unbelievable seventy-two degrees. On that rare day Big Bob said his arm got sunburned and the women all wore mini-skirts and shorts. Hard to picture in Barrow. The heat wave lasted precisely one day. The Arctic Ocean typically freezes for the winter in October and doesn't melt entirely until July so the surprisingly warm weather contrasted with a nearby frozen body of water.

I was lucky enough to be in Barrow for Nalukataq, the festival commemorating the end of the whaling season. On a mid-week festival day, offices were locked at noon and a large percentage of Inupiat residents shifted to the Browerville section of town. Charles Brower was the first white settler in Barrow before the turn of the century and not only does this neighborhood bear Brower's last name, so does a local store and a later generation of current residents. Whaling, before the beginning of the twentieth century, helped bring Lower 48 Americans and Europeans to Barrow. Some settled there.

During Nalukataq, families dressed in parkas or colorful, traditional overgarments called kuspuks, protecting themselves against a chill wind under a gray sky. People grouped together inside a three-sided, temporary canvas fencing as members of the successful whaling crew distributed muktuk, the blubbery part of the whale. It is local tradition that the whale is shared with all members of the community.

I took a few bites of muktuk and found the meat chewy and a little hard to swallow. Big Bob told me it would take a little while to get used to the taste. No adjustment of my taste buds was necessary to eat bearded seal. Back at the house, Martha Aiken's home-cooked stew dinner of seal, boiled potatoes and onions simmered in a large pan on the stove. The delicacy had a fishy quality, but was served much as spare ribs would be in a restaurant, meat still on the bone.

One feature of the whaling festival is a community blanket toss. A sealskin blanket, ringed with rope where it can be gripped, is pulled taut. A man or woman climbs up on the blanket and as the pullers relax and create tension on it the individual is thrust skyward. Hundreds of residents cheer. The blanket toss is perhaps the most familiar Native game to outsiders. It is simple, easy to catch on to, and it just looks like fun.

On my last night in town that trip, Big Bob drove me to the end of the road and onto the sandy shore outside town. His four nephews, aged four to twelve, rode in the back seat of his big car, absorbing every sight enthusiastically. We passed driftwood washed up from the sea, and the decaying carcasses of bowhead whales killed that spring. Harvested of their meat, they were merely black shells, rib cages resting in the water. Big Bob told me that in the middle of the light night, when all of the boaters go home and the shore road empties of cars, polar bears wander up and chew on the leftovers. I strained my eyes for a glimpse of a bear, but saw none.

Big Bob parked his big black Suburban and we clambered out. At this point of land, the Chukchi Sea and the Beaufort Sea meet. The sun was bright, the sky orange. We walked to within a few footsteps of the water.

"Welcome to the Top of the World," said Big Bob.

And welcome to the world of Big Bob, the World's Largest Eskimo.

—— Lew Freedman

Chapter 1

When I was a young man, before anyone ever called me Big Bob, I learned the Biblical legend of Jonah and the whale might be true.

Inupiat Eskimos hunt the bowhead whale off the Arctic Ocean near my home of Barrow, Alaska. Usually, we hunt in the springtime and when we go out and strike a whale with our harpoons tipped with explosive charges and are successful, there is great rejoicing in our community. The whale means a lot to us. It is part of our heritage and upbringing. Whenever a whaling crew kills a whale, everyone participates in hauling it to shore, in butchering it, and then savoring the taste of muktuk. It is a special event for the whole town.

However, I almost didn't live to learn and experience that. When I was fifteen, I was involved in a near-accident while whaling with some other teenaged relatives.

During that spring whaling season we put an outboard motor on our twenty-foot long umiaq, or skinboat. These are made from the skin of bearded seal stretched over a driftwood frame. At that time of year, the ocean is breaking up for the season and you can easily ram ice floes. With the motor we could steer more easily in and out of the ice chunks. There were many fast-moving icebergs since it was getting close to complete spring breakup. We are used to seeing this much loose ice every year and it can be very hazardous if you are not careful so we were just putt-putting along, not going very fast.

In many parts of the world, by the end of March it is starting to get warm, but where we live the air is still very cold, even below zero. That might last right on through April. It was night, but with bright sunshine. In spring, we also get gray, hazy days of fog when it is hard to see and I remember it had been that way right before. But the sunshine broke through.

We were maneuvering the boat and all of a sudden a whale rose right beside us. The whale broke the surface close by, its huge gray body rising and rising. I had seen this happen before, but never this close. When a whale cracks the surface of the water, it is something to see. It is like a big pane of glass breaking. The water pours off the whale's flanks like fragments of glass when they shatter. Very impressive. Soon, the whale was up to our boat's level, a few feet above the water. But it didn't stop there. The whale kept rising and rising. Higher and higher out of the water it came.

We were stunned. It must have been an eighty-foot whale! It was the biggest bowhead whale I ever saw and it was so close we could almost touch it.

I was so scared. We were supposed to be hunting whales, but this whale was too much for us to even think of capturing. It was so big it probably wasn't even aware we were there. To the whale, we were like a mosquito. It could just flick us away without even noticing. Really, to him, we would not even be as much of a bother as a mosquito to a human being.

If the whale had surfaced a few feet closer to the boat, it would have tipped us over. We might have drowned. We might even have frozen before we drowned. This was a monster whale. It could do anything it wanted to us and we would not even have interrupted his swimming path for a minute.

My first thought was, "We'd better get out of here." Our boat was so small next to it. We were a speck in the universe compared to a whale. It seemed to be turning towards us and it could have crushed us. And we couldn't run fast enough from a whale. They move so much faster than we could have to change direction. I looked up and we were so close that I was looking into this whale's great, huge eyeball. I saw the life in this great whale and it was so mighty it made me shiver.

Finally, the whale began to go back down under the water. Slowly, slowly, as slowly as it came up. It was just like a big submarine. And then it disappeared. It seemed like forever that it took it to come up and then go down. It was only five minutes, but it felt like a day or two.

We were hunting for whale and there was no way we could have killed this whale. It was the biggest whale I've ever heard of in all these years. I have never seen one bigger, though once I heard of one maybe seventy-five feet in Wainwright — almost as big.

I never saw this whale again and I would never want to cut him up. Too much work! We depend on whales for vitamins and minerals. They sustain the whole community, but this one, Whew! The hardest part of taking a whale is getting it on top of the ice once it is struck. I could not see how we would pull it up if we harpooned it. We don't usually even chase after whales we cannot capture.

That whale was big enough to put a Mack truck inside. Never mind me. Or Jonah.

The heaviest part of the whale is the tongue. The heaviest and the biggest organ. Whales eat plankton. They have these strainer-like teeth called baleen. The baleen has hairs on the end. They strain the plankton and swallow and spit out all this water and the hair traps the plankton they eat. The tongue creates this tremendous spit, or withdrawal of water.

And on this day, I pictured the whale knocking us flying out of our boat so easily and then sucking me up with that great tongue. I could have become Jonah. It was the most humbling experience.

That is the way we live in the north, in Barrow. There are many dangers and a hunter must be wise every time he leaves his home or there is no guarantee he will return. So many things can humble you.

My home in this part of Alaska is the coldest, harshest environment of all, where you will not live very long if you aren't fully prepared. We have the worst storms in the world in my hometown, with snow and wind blowing in from the sea, and temperatures so cold they will freeze you if you're not prepared and do not dress right. Even going for a walk just a little ways can be dangerous.

Whenever I have fear from the elements or animals around me I remember that I am an Inupiat Eskimo and my people have lived here for centuries. We have always lived a subsistence lifestyle, hunting the whales, the bearded seal, and also the ringed seal, moose, caribou, and sometimes even polar bears, if they come near us. We share this rugged land with the creatures of the north as best we can, but we depend on them as the source of our survival.

Sometimes the extreme cold that we deal with can overpower a man who is careless. And sometimes those creatures we live with are responsible for the death of a man. It happens. If the whale had captured me that day, I would not be the first who went out to hunt and did not come home.

It is part of the way of life here and it is not an easy way of life. But it is the way of life I have known. And it is the way of life that is our Eskimo upbringing. You cannot separate an Inupiat's values from the land. That is separating him from his culture, from his birthright.

We are the people of this part of the land and we choose to live here. And we thrive here among the whales, among the seals and the polar bears.

Chapter 2

If I was from another state or country and looked at a map and saw where Barrow was located, I suppose I'd wonder, "How does anybody live up there? What do they do in the wintertime?" They probably think, "That's a heck of a place to build a town."

Barrow is the farthest north town in the United States, located three-hundred-and-thirty miles above the Arctic Circle. That makes it pretty much far away from anyplace else, even in Alaska. Barrow is pretty much halfway between Alaska's capital of Juneau, which is in the southeastern part of the state, and the North Pole. You know, where Santa Claus hangs out. That North Pole, not the community in Alaska which has that name.

Not a lot of people know about Barrow because they barely see it on the map — it's usually just a dot — and it's so remote. Being way up north is the root of our identity, though.

The city is right on the spot where the Chukchi Sea from the west meets the Beaufort Sea from the east. Together those bodies of water form the Arctic Ocean. We're pretty far north any way you look at it. Someone said it's not the end of the world, but you can see it from there. In some ways they are right. When the ocean freezes off our shore that ice does lead to the end of the world.

Barrow is part of a government body called the North Slope Borough, which is like a county. But it must be the biggest county in the world. The borough has

89,000 square miles and to get an idea of how large that is, pull out a map of the United States and look at Minnesota. The North Slope Borough is about the same size as Minnesota.

The community of Barrow has about 4,100 people now, and that's about sixty percent of all the people who live in Alaska's North Slope Borough. By the mid-1990s Barrow was about twice as large as it was in 1980. Barrow has grown steadily in my lifetime. In the early 1950s, when I was born, Barrow had fewer than a thousand people and in those earliest years of my life maybe not more than two-hundred-and-fifty people.

The main expansion of Barrow began after 1980 and the growth has been pretty steady since. I don't know why we are so popular. It's still just as cold in the winter. I should explain that Barrow hasn't always been located exactly in the same place. Originally, Barrow was called Point Barrow, about twelve miles from where town is located now. It got started by hunters.

The people who came to Point Barrow, my ancestors, used to migrate to find food. They lived off the animals and they first came to Barrow to hunt snowy owls. That's how the settlement got its first name. Before we called it Barrow the place was called Ukpiaqvik. In the Inupiaq language that means "the place where people hunt snowy owls." Literally.

That goes back a long, long time. Then they moved away from Point Barrow to this new place. I think the first settlers kept getting hit by the violent storms that blow in off the water. So they looked for a new place inland that was not as exposed.

Of course, we are still the place of ice and snow and the environment is very harsh. A move of twelve miles did not eliminate that problem. Barrow is so cold that even in June you can see the sea ice right out the window of your house. There are not too many places in the United States where they can say that.

Barrow is known especially for where it is located geographically, but it is also known for a few other things. Everybody knows Barrow as the place where the plane crash in 1935 took the lives of the famous pilot Wiley Post and the famous writer Will Rogers. And there's the Naval Arctic Research Laboratory and we have a history that revolves around oil, too.

Long before it was said that oil was "discovered" on the North Slope and the oil companies set up their rigs in Prudhoe Bay, we heard stories about how our elders sometimes cut blocks of oil-soaked tundra and burned them for heat. Caribou hunters from Barrow would follow the herd east to Prudhoe Bay to hunt. When they camped along the way and built fires to cook their food and heat themselves in the tents, they chopped up pieces of the tundra that were so drenched in oil that they burned.

Barrow is a unique place and it is funny to watch visitors come to town who don't know much about it. Maybe they've just seen it on the map and think it would be interesting to go there. When they come around in the summer they wait for the sun to set so they can go to sleep. And they don't realize it never sets in the summer. So they stay up all night long, or until somebody tells them. Then they try to go to sleep with the sun still high up in the sky and they can't fall asleep unless they're exhausted.

It's nice to be from a place that is different. I could be from Omaha, Nebraska, or Wichita, Kansas, but I'd rather be from Barrow, from a town with a distinction of being so far north. It's a place where you hunt for your own table and can actually live off the land. Maybe they once hunted buffalo in those plains states, but I bet they don't feed themselves the hard way anymore.

Being from Barrow helps define who we are. Our Inupiat culture is so colorful. The things we do here in Barrow every day are so much a part of the way of life. We try to explain our history at all times to the younger generation and let young people know what the games are that we play and the emotion we bring to our motion dances. To some stranger who observes Eskimo customs without any background it may just be games and dances, but to our children it is a unique and colorful heritage.

Passing on cultural history through stories and games that represent the subsistence lifestyle and even dances is an Inupiat tradition. It becomes clear just how important those things are when you realize there is something else hidden within the games and dances about who we are. A lot of the stories told revolve around where we come from. To a large degree, I am a self-educated man. Meaning that I learned less from formal schooling and books than from the words of my elders.

If you live in Barrow you had better be somebody who likes cold weather. On a given day in the summer it might only be thirty degrees above zero. On some days it is even colder. We might get snow flurries on the first day of summer. I think most Americans would say that is winter, not summer, but we're used to it. Since I have grown up with this kind of weather, it's fine. Being from Barrow, I can't stand the hot weather.

Once, I visited Arizona in the summer and it was a hundred-and-ten degrees. Man, I tell you, I felt like a snow man that might melt in a few minutes. My blood is filled up with so much anti-freeze that I don't suffer from the freezing cold in the winter in Barrow. So when you are not used to that Arizona type of heat, Whew! I try to avoid that kind of heat, especially direct hot sun.

A lot of people don't understand that once in a while it gets very hot up north. For us in Barrow, if we have a few days when the temperature is as high as seventy, that's something else. We can take our coats off for a change.

But that's nothing. Inland, where my fish camp is located, it actually gets to be ninety degrees. One time I got stuck out there when it was scorching hot like that, but it didn't overwhelm me because I was too bothered by mosquitoes to notice. The mosquitoes can swarm you in such numbers and with such fierceness that the temperature is the least of your worries. Also, in towns like Fort Yukon which are also above the Arctic Circle, it gets as hot as ninety sometimes. The heat doesn't last very long, but it happens. People can't believe it.

If you live in Barrow, not only must you get used to cold, you must get used to darkness around the clock in the winter and sunlight for twenty-four hours in the summer. The sun rises above the horizon in May and doesn't set until August. In the winter, the sun sets in November and doesn't rise again until the end of January.

I grew up with all that daylight in the summer, so I'm used to it. I can fall asleep outside in the brightness. It doesn't matter to me if it is light out. I just feel sorry for people who can't fall asleep when they come to Barrow. They think it's not normal for the sun to stay out in the sky so late, but to us it's normal.

When we were kids we wanted to stay up late, all night long. We felt we should be allowed to run around playing all we wanted until it got dark, that it was our right. Not everyone did. In the old days, we got chased by the local Mothers' Club. They wanted us to go home by midnight. If you're a kid out playing you ignore the clock.

It's harder for everyone to get used to the darkness of winter, even when you have lived in Barrow all your life. We can cope with it better than most people, of course, but we do choose to go out of town a lot in the winter. Some people schedule regular winter vacations to Hawaii. When I can I go to Anchorage or Fairbanks for a break in the winter. That's fun for me to go to the bigger cities in Alaska.

When it's dark and you're used to a lot of activity you get lonely for just going outdoors and seeing a little bit of daylight. It seems like every time you go out you're looking for the sun. I hardly notice the sun during the summer when it's out all the time, except for how bright the day might be. There are too many activities. But in the winter, that's all you think about — When is the sun going to come back?

My favorite part of the summer is when I can go boating. In winter, we are hemmed in by a solid sheet of ice. Come springtime the ice cracks and breaks up and large chunks float nearby. The icebergs are still there for a while, but usually you can go around them. The ice is out completely only for about ten or so weeks of the year in July, August and September. For months, just offshore it's frozen solid.

We time the fall whale hunt for just before freeze-up. You want to go out just before the ice comes in, at the coldest time, so when you get a whale it won't rot by the time you bring it in to shore. You want to keep it chilled.

Summer in Barrow is not like summer anywhere else. First, there are only those ten weeks when the ocean is water, not ice. We may get long hours of sunshine, but it can be windy, too, so you still need a coat. The best thing about the wind is that when it's blowing with any strength it mostly keeps the mosquitoes away. Don't count on the wind to help you out if you go inland, though. Then you will run into mosquitoes by the thousands. Also, if you see caribou, you will see the mosquitoes. They follow the animals. Talk about vampires.

We have stretches when the temperature will reach into the fifties and stay there for several days. That's nice. The Arctic sun feels warmer than the temperature reads. Boy, we get ultraviolet rays. The sun is strong. The rays are tremendous. When you are exposed to them in white snow, you get sun-blind and if you are not careful the rays will get to your eyes and keep them dry.

When the temperature goes to seventy, that's too much, too intense. It's pretty rare, but when it happens it boils my blubber. It only happens once every few years, though. And only for one day at a time, usually. Our elders say that if it's a very cold winter it will be a warm summer.

You should be in Barrow when it's seventy degrees. It's the topic of the whole town. Imagine being somewhere else when a big snowstorm hits, or when cold weather of twenty degrees below zero arrives. That's all people talk about. When it gets warm in Barrow, that's all anybody there talks about. The elders are talking about it. It will be all over the citizen's band radio how strange it is.

We spend a lot of time getting ready for winter, but we don't prepare for a warm summer.

Fall really begins in August and freeze-up comes fast after that. We are all feverishly trying to get ready for winter, gathering caribou meat and bearded seal. We get the sealskins ready for the boats. We go after walrus, hunt some ducks. It's pretty mild then. To me, mild is thirty-five or forty degrees.

It rains more in July and August. The caribou are getting fat, walrus are starting to pass the Point, headed towards Canada, and the bearded seals have pretty much gone away to the north. At the same time we are trying to get ahead it starts raining, raining, raining.

By October in Barrow we are really focused on preparing for winter. It's time to begin storing a lot of our summer stuff away. All the activity is focused on whaling again in September and October. We seem to get the biggest monster whales in the fall.

Maybe because it's the end of the summer and winter is coming fast, or maybe because hunting whales in the fall is a more recent tradition, since the coming of the outboard motor, but there is no whaling celebration festival in the fall, no blanket toss at the end of fall whaling.

After fall whaling, we clean up the boats, dry-dock them. And then once November arrives, the sun sets and we're into winter. Everything is dead calm. We are waiting for final freeze-up. In the early months of winter, October and November, before the ocean freezes for good, you can go ice fishing. You catch a lot of whitefish and trout then. Maybe some ling cod if you're lucky. Then you might get some caribou. You put it all away, the meat and fish, to eat in wintertime.

By January, everything stops. Nobody moves around much in Barrow then. It's as if the community, not only the ocean, is frozen in place. If people don't go away on trips, they hardly have any activities. In February and March, your mind starts drifting to spring whaling. I like that time of year. The sun is up and you feel the new season is beginning. There is excitement in the spring air.

There can be such a thing as too much excitement, though.

In May of 1997 we experienced a terrifying event. While most of our expert whale hunters were out on the Chukchi Sea, a twenty-mile sheet of ice cracked open and began drifting away. There were one-hundred-and-forty-two hunters trapped on the ice, separated from land and in danger of being swept away and killed.

I could easily have been among those who were out on the ice. Some of my uncles were there. But at the time I was sixty-five miles inland hunting geese instead. I usually would be whale hunting with them, but for some reason I didn't want to go. I had a sense that I should stay home, stay off the ice. Just a feeling.

The whalers had all of their gear, their skinboats and snowmachines, out on the ice with them. Whalers who were members of more than twenty of our crews were out there and there was tremendous potential for tragedy. Normally, we are very aware of the ice conditions and the chances for the ice to break off like that, but this time everyone was caught off-guard.

I have been out there when the ice broke. It's a very uncomfortable feeling when you have a crack behind you. When a crack turns to a break, it closes off your lifeline. Man, it's a weird, scary feeling. Those whalers knew there was a crack that could go beyond the comfort zone. When the ice snapped, they were all in trouble. The sheet of ice began drifting out to the open sea and they were thirty-five miles offshore before help came.

That was a big rescue. It was foggy, but it was possible to get helicopters in the air and they were able to take the whale hunters off the ice one by one. Everyone might have died, but nobody got hurt. Some of the crews lost all of their whaling equipment, though, and that can cost $10,000.

It was luck that no one got hurt, or that nobody got crushed by the ice. It was a miracle. Most of the people around Barrow are praying people. We were all praying. A sense of hopelessness set in briefly for some of them, but all of the whalers got back.

Even the most experienced hunters were surprised this happened to them. It took a couple of days for some to get picked up. They didn't know what would happen. Being on an ice floe for a long time like that will make you very worried. The hunters were lucky enough to have a handheld Global Positioning System unit with them. That was the single biggest thing that helped in the rescue. It made a big difference. After the crack split the ice wide open the fog rolled in, but the rescuers could use the GPS to track them.

Some of the hunters knew they barely got out alive and many members of the community were in shock for a long time afterwards.

To be honest, there was one good, tangible reason I went hunting inland instead of out onto the ice whaling. Our elders warned us about the conditions. I listen to my elders. They tell me to be aware of things and to be alert. That crack was there most of the spring. Our hunters just got too comfortable with things and they went out anyway.

Even later, the elders were saying, "We told you so."

We always should listen to our elders. Our elders have the experience and they know what they are doing. I always knew that, even when I was a young man, but I didn't always follow their wisdom.

When I was a boy, and later a young man, my elders were always attempting to educate me, to tell me things that would help me in life. But I was rebellious and often I let the advice roll off of me. That is part of the growing process, I guess. It took me a long time to learn that education is important and is a continuous process.

When you are young and full of yourself, you aren't always smart enough to listen to the elders. I made that mistake many times over. It took me a long time to get educated, to understand that my elders were trying to help me out.

When we're young, we don't pay attention. When we get into a tough spot and the elders say, "I told you so," it's for a reason. We're headstrong. We think we know everything.

Our elders say you are never too old to learn. Every day I learn something new.

Chapter 3

I was born April 15, 1953 in Barrow Hospital. My dad used to work there doing maintenance, for years, and he was right there when I was born. Given the time of year it was, I probably interrupted his spring whaling.

I was one of eleven boys and girls in the Aiken family. Ten of them were born to Robert and Martha Aiken and one was adopted. All of the members of my family who have survived stayed in Barrow except one sister. Vera, who is the youngest, got married and moved to Southeast Alaska.

Growing up in Barrow was a lot of fun. If you were a kid in the 1950s and 1960s, there was so much to do. Not the same kind of things kids do nowadays, though. All my brothers, Percy, Joseph, Earl, Percy K., John, and I, were best friends. We all grew up in a big house on the beach. Or at least it seemed big to us then.

Boy, we used to run around. In most parts of the United States, kids play outdoors in the sun and warmth. To us it was normal to be outside doing things when it was zero degrees, or even twenty degrees below zero. Most of the time we didn't care too much about cold weather. That was our world.

When I was about seven years old, we'd go hunting for birds with slingshots. We made our own slingshots. The rubber came from old tires, blown out tires. We'd cut the rubber into strips and stretch it. The rubber on the inner tubes was real stretchy. We made the handles from driftwood that washed ashore from who knows how many thousands of miles away. We'd search the beach for the right shaped driftwood, in a V shape. Good handles for slingshots.

And the way we'd attach the rubber and the wood was by cutting up dental floss and a piece of sealskin, or caribou skin, and shaving the hair off. The skin was like a sling for us. When we had tied it all off, we'd made slingshots.

Our ammunition was the rocks we found on the beach. That way we never ran out of ammunition. I was very young, so I didn't even know the names of the birds, but we got pretty good at hitting them. A lot of us got good at it. On some days we could hit them from fifty feet. But on other days we'd miss and we'd have to get right up on them. We'd creep right up on the birds, very quietly, and shoot them. Then we'd bring them home.

I was usually a very good shot. I didn't know that I would become a good hunter until much later when I owned a boat, but I guess you could say I showed some early signs of being able to kill game. I hit quite a few birds. It's a case where something you're playing at has important meaning for what you do later in life. What was play leads to something serious.

One time a bumblebee came around and I was very scared of it. I thought it would sting me. It was about ten feet away from me and I shot at it with a rock from my slingshot and I hit it! Just when it landed. I just aimed and shot. I didn't really mean to hit it, just scare it away, but I actually hit it. Wow!

There were no witnesses around, just me. So when I told my brothers, they didn't believe me. True story, though. I only shot at the bee because it frightened me.

I remember we used to trade some birds for pieces of crackers. There was an old man who used to eat the birds and he gave us crackers. Those Sailor Boy crackers. People all over the north kind of lived on those. They're hard and unsalted and come in big boxes. We ate a million of them when I was a kid.

I tried eating one of the birds one time. We roasted it. We were on our way home and stopped to build a fire. We were a long ways from town and we were walking back and got very hungry. Snack time. We took the feathers off and plucked it and then we put it on the end of a stick. It tasted mighty good, but there wasn't very much of it. It wasn't very filling. It was too small. I guess it was like pheasant or quail, delicacies you might find on the menu in fancy restaurants some places. But those people don't kill their dinner themselves.

The Sailor Boy crackers filled you up. Those crackers have been around Barrow a long time. The old whalers, who came from New England and from Europe, traveling thousands of miles, used to carry the crackers with them on their journeys because they didn't spoil. They are packaged well and they get shipped by boat and stay fresh a long, long time. They have quite a history in the

Arctic.

We always had crackers, but when I was a kid the ships used to dock and the sailors would get off and bring in a whole bunch of goodies for us. They usually gave us hard rock candy as a treat. They probably had so much of it because it kept well, too, on their long voyages.

Now kids have so many toys and things, but when I was a kid, the cliffs on the edge of town overlooking the Arctic Ocean were our playground. There was soft, drifted snow on the cliffs and we made tunnels and made hideouts where we'd play. We made igloos to play in.

People still always ask if we live in igloos. That's just ignorance. Eskimos never lived in igloos. The igloos my brothers and sisters made together might be like tree houses kids built in their backyards in other places in the Lower 48.

Those tunnels were pretty deep and they'd go a long, long ways, all over the cliffs. We'd play tag in the tunnels. We'd run through the tunnels like lemmings, chasing each other. The tunnels never collapsed. The roof would get super hard because of the cold. It could hold a lot of weight. The drifting snow compacts in the wind. It gets real hard, real fast in the winter. Blown snow holds together and becomes harder than fallen snow.

When we got tired of that, we'd start jumping off the cliffs right on top of the soft snow to see who could go the deepest into the snow. Sometimes we would sink way down, clear up over our heads. We would have to dig our way out.

Another thing I did with my brothers was explore. We would go for miles out of town, all along the shore, almost to Point Barrow, twelve miles away. When you grow up in the big city, you might never leave your little neighborhood, but to us the whole area was our town. There were very few strangers in Barrow when we were kids. We never even thought about getting in trouble with a stranger.

My brothers and sisters always enjoyed each other. We enjoyed going to places to see other families and playing with other kids, or relatives. I have a lot of cousins. But they were second best because our brothers and sisters were the best. We were just constantly doing things together. Those were the days when we were so close we would never go anywhere without each other. Only later, as we grew up and went to work and started to earn our keep did we start to drift apart. Most of my brothers and sisters have their own families and other obligations now.

Robert, my dad, set the rules for us. I'm sure parents everywhere have rules of behavior their kids must follow. In cities, they tell you not to cross the street when cars are coming. In our region, we had to be very aware of a different kind of environment.

We'd get scolded a lot if we did too much exploring. Dad would warn us about dangers. Stay away from this. Stay away from that. He told us not to walk too far from town, and he told us not to smoke cigarettes.

My dad never really punished us much, though. He lectured us and scolded us if we did wrong, but he hardly ever hit us. He is a special dad. Most of the kids I knew got a real whipping if they acted up. When my dad was serious, he did get it across plainly never to do something again. Just behave.

My mom, Martha, warned us to be careful of polar bears. Good advice. Polar bears often come up on the beach and they do come into town sometimes. But we were having so much fun exploring we didn't think much about it. I never remember seeing a polar bear when we were out as kids roaming around. Now that I think back we could have been in danger, so we were lucky.

One of my uncles shot a polar bear outside of town at the Naval Arctic Research Laboratory in the 1960s. He shot this big bear and it turned out it was a mother who had two cubs. He realized it when the cubs came running out from hiding and discovered that their mother was dead. He brought the cubs into town and for a little while he kept them in his backyard. Not very many people ever have polar bear cubs as pets, even for a little while. I used to go look at them all the time. I just kept staring at them. I was taken with them. Cute little things. So fluffy and so beautiful.

After about a week my uncle gave them to the Research Lab. They had all the animals of the north up there, polar bears, wolves, porcupines, caribou, reindeer. I even remember seeing an eagle. In fact, there were two eagles.

My parents tried to teach us to respect the cold and the harsh weather of winter. We didn't always listen, though. Up until a certain age we were only concerned with the games we played. But gradually we understood we had to be careful. Every time we went out, we'd have to put on clothing that would keep us warm all day. We were never supposed to go outside without gloves on, or a parka, or mukluks on our feet.

We were taught to watch after our brothers and sisters. To make sure to keep an eye on them. Don't lose sight of them, we were told. When the wind was blowing we had to hold hands when we went out to visit neighbors. When it was cold my parents always asked where we were going, what we were going to do. And they would always say, "Don't go too far." They would tell us all the time that you could easily get lost or easily freeze. The temperature could go as low as fifty degrees below zero and with a strong wind it would even feel colder than that.

They taught us not to fear the cold, but to be watchful. And always to be careful if the wind started blowing. If we were on the water we were to come right home if the wind was blowing. The wind could make it feel like a hundred degrees below zero. It would go right through you. Brr. That was cold.

Chapter 4

I am an Inupiat Eskimo, but some of my ancestors come from Ireland.

That's the origin of my last name. It's pronounced A-Kin, but once there was an old man in town who took to calling me "I-Gun." He said my last name, "I-Gun." So I finally asked him one day why he called me that and he said that was my great-grandfather's name.

It wasn't until I was about twenty-five years old that I even thought about the Irish portion of my heritage. I think my family was just involved in the Inupiat culture and wasn't really curious about the Irish part. Once, though, probably in the early part of the twentieth century, an Irish whaler came to Barrow and this stranger is part of my family history.

I think he came with some men who got stranded here on a whaling vessel, or their whaling boat got crushed by the ice and they had no choice but to live in Barrow. The early whalers, that's where a lot of well-known Barrow names came from: the Hobsons, the Leavitts and the Aikens. My ancestor might have been a trader or a whaler, I'm not completely sure which.

My father, Robert, was born in 1929. His father was Johnny Aiken. The great-grandfather before him was the one who came to Barrow that we don't know much about. It was possible it was in the 1890s. But I was raised as an Inupiat all the way and we were never told about our Irish background. For a while a relative of ours named Floyd Aiken was coming up to visit us from Florida and I knew about him, so I understood there were Aikens in other places. There were also some African-Americans named Aiken and that got me even more curious. How were we related?

After high school and into my twenties I started to have some curiosity about that branch of the family, about exploring my heritage more specifically. One day I got a letter in the mail that said if you want to know about your past you can sign up. I started thinking that there must still be some family back in Ireland. Me and my cousins talked about it and thought maybe we ought to go over there some time. But we never got around to it.

It would have been interesting. That would be something to discover the other side of yourself. It also would have been very interesting to see how people would react to me if I went there and introduced myself as an Eskimo who was a descendant of an Aiken who was a whaler from Northern Ireland.

My whole upbringing was Inupiat Eskimo, though. I think my parents and uncles didn't want to talk about Irish connections because for years people were cut down as half-breeds. So we lived a wholly Inupiat way of life. I consider myself to be a full-blooded Inupiat. And I think that is what my aunts and uncles and parents would want me to be.

I learned the Inupiat way. It was up to me how much I wanted to listen and pay attention. My grandfather on my mother's side, Vincent Nageak, played a part in that. He didn't speak much in English, but he was really concerned that we behaved the proper way, that we shouldn't be unruly kids. If he saw something he didn't like that we were doing he would say, "That's not right!"

There were times I was a very good listener and absorbed what he said. There were times I thought I was listening, but went off and did what I felt like. I think most kids are like that.

My grandpa was a whaling captain for years and he was highly respected. He was also well-known as a polar bear hunter. Skinning polar bears turned his hair white, I think. And his skin turned white. Everything on him turned white because of one incident when he was in his sixties. He was cutting up a polar bear he killed and scraped a piece of liver. Some hunters cleaned their knives by licking them. They licked the oil off to sharpen them. He licked his knife once and part of the oil from the bear's liver got in his bloodstream. His skin turned a white pink. You could never tell he was Inupiat. He looked like a white man.

From the time I was a little boy until I was seven or so, I would sit at his knee in the living room of his house and listen to him tell story after story about whaling and polar bear hunting and survival in the elements. My grandma and aunts and uncles would be too busy to sit down. I'd be the only one listening, it seemed. He wanted to pass on his wisdom and knowledge to me. He told me the right equipment to take when I went seal hunting or anywhere out on the ice and taught me respect.

It is Inupiat custom to pass on wisdom from generation to generation this way. Later, I appreciated it more than I did when I was a rebellious teenager.

One time, my grandpa told me that he fell in the freezing water and the ice was moving with the current, against the wind. He was by himself in the water and the ice was coming at him real fast. Somehow he heaved himself up on the ice. With a heavy parka that's almost impossible. He said the way he did it was to throw one arm onto the lip of the ice and throw one leg up, then roll right onto the ice.

He always said never to go out on the ice without a manuq, a coil of string that has a hook at the end. A couple of times the manuq came in real handy for him. When he was drifting out to sea on the current, he threw the hook onto the ice to pull himself back in.

These were life and death situations. He'd be sitting out on the ice by the edge of the water and all of a sudden, a jerk, and he would guess he was drifting out. For some reason the ice suddenly moves like that. Either a big ice floe just breaks loose while you're sitting on it, or a piece of ice hits the main ice pack and causes it. That's when you'd better head for shore fast.

I'd picture in my mind what I would do if that was me in those circumstances.

Grandpa was a very influential man in my life. Anything that came from grandpa was very serious. I think that every time he spoke he chose the words wisely. Every time he spoke, he wanted to help you in some way to see how near-fatal incidents could happen and instruct you how to avoid them.

Everything about him was gentle, the way he talked, even the way he said, "That's not right!" He was telling me some of the same things my parents said. I remember dad telling me that if you sit around too much you will get sick. I thought he was just kidding. I laughed at that. But grandpa told me that if you sit around too much you get fat, lazy and die. Later, I realized if I stopped moving I did start getting sick.

When I first started to show an interest in playing the Native games, my grandpa told me that these were not just games I was playing. "They are going to help you," he said. I didn't know what he meant then, but it was absolutely true.

All of the Native games that are contested in the World Eskimo-Indian Olympics illustrate a purpose. Each event has a story behind it that relates to our culture and our subsistence way of life.

My first exposure to the Native games was in Barrow. We have the Christmas games every year as part of the holiday celebration. But when I was growing up you had to be sixteen years old in order to compete. The games were for the grown men and I watched them do the stick pull and wrestle and do the high kick.

I was always curious about these games. I always looked forward to Christmas. Probably the first game I got to play was the finger pull. I did it with my dad. You hook forefingers around each other's and pull until the finger is straight. Or someone gives up. Most people give up when the pulling starts to hurt. You do it first with the right hand, then with the left. It's two-out-of-three to see who wins. My dad always won.

We did the stick pull, too. You sit on the floor, facing your opponent, and place the stick between the two of you, grab onto it, and try to pull it away from the other person. My dad beat me at that, too. In fact, my dad and my uncles were always dominating the games in Barrow. They were all muscle. I was not old enough to participate, but I was naturally big enough so I was desperate to start competing with other men of the community.

I was so big that not everybody around realized exactly how old I really was. When I was fourteen late in 1967, I easily could pass for sixteen. I looked even older than that. I don't know why my dad didn't say something. I think he saw the fire in my eyes, that I wanted to be in the games. For a long time I was right there alongside my dad, watching when there was a game on, or when disputes would arise about how the games were being played. I was learning.

Every time my uncles did strength games they would show off. They were all muscle, every one of them and they would win in the Eskimo stick pull, the finger pull, the arm pull, and wrestling. I wanted to try most of the games, but I was especially impressed with them in wrestling. If I tried it, I thought they would hurt me, that they would throw me around like a rag doll. I was unsure about that event.

In Eskimo wrestling, the object of the game is to put your opponent onto his back with you on top of him. Outdoors, you're standing up, facing each other and hugging. Indoors, you start on your knees, face-to-face, chest-to-chest. And you lock arms and try to pin your opponent on his back on the floor. The first one to pin two-out-of-three is the winner.

The wrestling started as a friendly competition among our local whalers to show off their strength. My uncle taught me technique. But like all of the other games, it is something important to our culture beyond just sport. Wrestling like this helps you to be strong and alert and be in control. I think by learning the technique and quick reflexes, it helps us in life in unforeseen instances.

Also, those who selected members of the whaling crews would want to know how strong you were. They might want you in their crew if you had the strength. It could be beneficial for the captain of the boat to have strong and able-bodied men. Strength and reflexes and quick thinking is what's required for all subsistence hunting.

In the arm pull, the competitors sit face-to-face, lock arms, then for leverage, grab their opponent's foot. It's like the finger pull. You pull until the arm straightens out or the grip slips off. Faces strain and grimace and if you hang on too long you can injure a bicep. During competition my uncles would show off how strong they were by intimidation. They'd shake their arms playing as if they'd been hurt, and try to intimidate others. See you next year, they'd be saying. Or, Come back when you're older and wiser.

When that happened, it was definitely embarrassing because all the relatives were watching. I would say it is mildly effective if your uncle is doing that to you. Yes, indeed, the mental aspect is part of the games. Of course, at the Christmas games, it's mostly play, among friends. At the World Eskimo-Indian Olympics we don't pose or do anything like that. It could be misunderstood unless those around you are close friends.

The Eskimo stick pull reflects brute strength. The idea is to take the two-foot-long stick away from your opponent two out of three times, as well. This game mimicks seal hunters, I believe. When the seal hunters in the old days went out on the ice to look for breathing holes with a harpoon and struck a seal when it was coming up for air, the reflex of that seal would be to go back down the breathing hole. These bearded seals are very big, maybe eight feet long and a thousand pounds or more, and they are very powerful.

The hunter is hanging on to the harpoon, which is tied to a rope, and he has to lift the seal out of the water as it struggles. This is a lot easier to say than to do. You get in a tug-of-war with the seal. Once you start pulling out a seal you never give up. You just keep pulling. You can rest for a little while because the harpoon across the breathing hole is a stopper and it would have to break for the seal to go down so far you can't get it. The rope was sealskin cut into strips and dried. It is really strong rope. You could pull a truck out of the water with that kind of strap.

If you are strong enough, you will pull the seal out above the ice. Even if the seal dies below the water, you have all that weight to pull through a small hole.

The stick pull may be a game, but it has a real-life aspect.

I was fourteen years old and I thought I was strong in my first Christmas games. I did pretty well in those events in the early rounds like some of my older friends, but then when we got near the finals I was going up against my uncles and I was the one who got intimidated. Us young bucks were working hard all the way and my uncles had saved their strength for the end. They'd hold back and we didn't know any better, but they knew that was the way to do it. We would wear ourselves out and the older men would get the points. They had the experience and wisdom of their years.

That was the way my uncles worked. If it wasn't for them, I wouldn't be nearly as good a heavy equipment operator for the North Slope Borough now. My uncle Jonathan Aiken would tell me I wasn't really an operator on my road grader, but just someone who drives around. He motivated me to get better at everything, including using equipment, by using reverse psychology.

Uncle Jonathan beat me in the arm pull and the finger pull in the games for years. He'd squeeze the blood out of my fingers. And then he'd tell me I wasn't a man yet. But I learned things from that first time. I learned technique and I learned the mental aspects and I learned that intimidating your opponent can be important. You can psyche him out and save energy.

Getting beat at the Christmas games the first year was the driving force for me to get better for the next time.

It took me a little while to learn the lesson of motivation my uncles were trying to teach me and to understand they were using reverse psychology. My grandma Rhoda Nageak did the same thing. She would sit me down and put me to work sewing the tears on sleeping bags, or whatever needed repairing with needle and thread. For years, I thought she was just being mean. For years. But one day well after high school when I was living alone and had to sew my own patches I realized she was just trying to help me. She wanted me to be self-sufficient, to be able to fend for myself.

She was actually teaching me survival skills, how to survive on my own when my family would not be there to help me.

And after that first Christmas games when my uncles hung me out to dry, they helped me tremendously. They told me I was improving, that I was getting stronger and I was on the right path. In the beginning, they didn't want me to get a swelled head. When I got older and got to be a better athlete they treated me as an equal and no longer tried to intimidate me.

It took me a few years, but by the time I was eighteen I started to win the strength events at the Christmas games. The first event I ever won was the Eskimo stick pull, but it took time to build up the endurance to go through all the rounds. I remember one time some skin peeled off the palms of my hands from doing so many stick pulls and I had to quit because they hurt so much. I had to build up callouses. It took from age fourteen to eighteen before I could beat the top guy. It took me a long time to get to that next level.

But by the time I was twenty-five I was dominating. By then I was bigger than all of them, too.

Chapter 5

Even though my brothers and I were explorers at heart and it didn't bother us to play outside in the dark, wind and snow, that kind of weather still kept us indoors more often as kids than happens in most other places. Our parents made sure of that.

Since we were inside a lot, that's one reason why I think my brothers and sisters were so close. We had to entertain ourselves. We listened to a lot of music — I like all kinds of music and particularly old rock and roll. And we listened to our parents and relatives and their visitors tell stories about our people, sometimes for hours.

Some of what we heard were silly stories. My favorite was the one a great uncle told about a ten-legged polar bear. He said it was a true story, not a myth. He said he saw it walking along the ice and it was so big it fell through real thick ice. I believed him.

Like any kid, I thought my town was the only place in the world. Barrow was it. We didn't have television in the early 1950s. Hearing stories from my family was the first I realized that there were even other villages someplace. I heard there were other people, in other places, who lived differently. But when I thought about a different place I really thought my parents meant they were people who were camping, not living in another town. I didn't think there could be another town like Barrow.

Finally, when I was about eight or nine years old I realized that when the airplane landed in Barrow people with strange faces got off. They had to come from somewhere. That's when I really knew there was another Barrow out there.

And then when we got television I also learned that not everyplace was just like Barrow. I found out there were warmer places, that there were places where people wore short sleeves! And had bigger houses and fancy cars. Plus, I watched American Bandstand. American Bandstand was one of those shows we never missed. There weren't any Eskimos on American Bandstand that I saw.

I always did like all kinds of music. It started with my parents. They would invite people from the Presbyterian Church to come by and they'd sing religious songs all the way into the wee hours of the morning. I was raised Presbyterian. I went to Sunday school and vacation Bible school in the summer, though we never really went anywhere far away.

Bible camp was one thing, but by the time I was about eleven, I remember the whole family going inland to camp on the Colville River. In springtime, late April or early May, we went hunting to get meat to feed the family. The days were getting longer, but there was still plenty of snow on the ground. We'd take the dog team, or later, a snowmachine. It was a trip of about fifty miles. In summer, after breakup, when the ice went out, we'd go down the coast in one of our wooden boats that we sometimes used for whaling. They're about twenty-five feet long and open to the air. They had oars, but you could also put up a sail.

That's how we were traveling the time I almost lost my father. My whole family was going caribou hunting, though I was still too young to shoot a gun. My dad was hunting for all of us and my uncle Jimmy Aiken, his brother, was along. We set up camp in Beard Bay and when a storm hit us kids were told to stay in the tent.

The wind was howling and the surf was getting real high, making the boat drift out on the waves. My mother was already in the boat and my dad was trying to retrieve it. He was reaching for the rope and he got caught by the current. The water was moving so fast he got swept under and my uncle had to pull him out by the hair. He was completely under water. Even when the sun has been out for months, the water in the Arctic never gets very warm, and in the spring the temperature is barely above freezing.

It was very cold out when they brought my dad into the tent and he was really, really shivering. He almost died of hypothermia. They turned up the gas stove so high and made it so hot I had to go out of the tent.

I was very frightened. I thought I was losing my dad. But the next morning he was okay and I was so relieved.

Up until I was in my mid-teenage years, there were a lot of sled dog teams in Barrow. My uncle Jimmy had a team and we could borrow the dogs and take rides just for fun. He had nine or ten dogs and boy, those were big dogs. These days, the huskies the mushers use to run the Iditarod Trail Sled Dog Race weigh about fifty pounds each, but these dogs were much bigger. I remember they had really big feet. I think they were part wolf.

My uncles were the dog drivers. I just rode along when we went to the dump to get ice for melting, or to get empty barrels there. Just for errands. I had so much fun riding in those days when I was little — it would have been harder work for the dogs to pull me when I weighed five hundred pounds.

But then I had a bad experience with dogs and I never really liked dog sleds after that. I ran into a bunch of dogs in somebody else's yard. They were tied up, but some broke loose and they were all barking at me and surrounded me. I didn't know where to go. I was terrified and started running and ran right into a pole. Boy, that hurt. After that I had nothing to do with dog sleds.

Until the mid-1960s, dog teams were a big part of life in Barrow. Dogs are very popular in Alaska now because of the Iditarod and other big races, but we relied on dogs for transportation, not sport. When I was about fourteen, my dad bought our first snowmachine and that was a big highlight.

We loved driving that snowmachine fast. We volunteered to do all the chores, get ice, go to the dump, whatever. It was, "Dad, we'll do it for you." We looked for every opportunity to go snowmachining.

And just like that, by 1970 or so, dog teams were gone. They were totally replaced. The only dogs left were for pets. Some people kept some husky dogs, just in case a snowmachine broke down. The shift was fairly fast as the machines kept improving. Everybody just went out and bought a snowmachine, or traded something for one. They were a lot faster than dogs — they can go eighty miles an hour — and they can haul a lot heavier load of caribou.

Now once more there are a few dog teams in Barrow, but twenty years or so ago the snowmachine coming represented a big lifestyle change. It must have been like when the railroad crossing the Lower 48 came along and replaced the horse.

Chapter 6

I am now six feet, four inches tall and weigh three-hundred-and-thirty pounds. But earlier in my adult life I weighed as much as five hundred pounds. I got so much attention for being big that I actually was approached by the World Wrestling Federation to join up.

Can you imagine me as a professional wrestler?

One day some time in the early 1980s, I picked up the telephone and it was this lady from Seattle calling. She said she was representing big-time wrestling and they wanted to send someone to Barrow to interview me.

This was the kind of wrestling you see on television all the time, those guys with the nicknames who throw people around the ring and bounce them off the canvas. The Iron Sheik, Sgt. Slaughter, Hulk Hogan. Who knows what they would have tried to name me? Probably the Eskimo Savage.

I don't know how they heard about me. Maybe they saw a show about the World Eskimo-Indian Olympics on television. I was at my biggest then, about five hundred pounds, so that might have made an impression on them.

I was a little bit curious, but I didn't really want any part of the World Wrestling Federation. For a while I thought it must be some kind of prank or something. She kept calling me, though. Once she said she was in Anchorage and was coming up to see me. I was on my way to fish camp, though, and I left town.

I never saw her.

I wasn't hurting for money at the time and I never was that kind of wrestler. I really wasn't that interested. On television the wrestling looked like one big, phony thing and everybody thinks it's fake to this day. I didn't want to be part of that. I wouldn't want to reach kids that way.

No doubt I was big enough for them, though. My bones are heavy. Even as a child I had heavy bones.

I was a pretty big kid, though I grew a lot more later. Actually, when I was a young youngster, before I was the world's biggest Eskimo, my older brother John was bigger than me. For just a little while. I really was a little guy once. There was a picture of me and my grandma and my older brother and I was holding a real big Sugar Daddy that seemed as big as me. They made that candy really big in those days. It took me months to finish that. Then I started to grow up. I don't think there's any candy out there now that's bigger than me.

Eventually, I grew up to be bigger than all my uncles, bigger than anyone in Barrow, bigger than any other Eskimo. The world's largest Eskimo. That's me.

By the time I was about eighteen years old, I was six feet tall and weighed about two hundred-and-fifty pounds. But I kept growing. By the time I was twenty-five years old I weighed more than three hundred pounds. And I was a strong three hundred pounds.

It would be nice to tell you that it was so, but all that weight wasn't always all muscle. As time passed, I kept getting bigger and bigger. In my thirties, when I weighed five hundred pounds, I was very obese. I was always strong, but I was a heavy drinker and a heavy smoker at that time. The drinking is all behind me, though I do still like to eat. I did earn the name Big Bob, that's for sure.

The first time I truly realized that I was pretty strong I was about sixteen years old. I picked up a metal gas can with handles and threw it at my brother Earl. When I turned around I saw him lying on the ground. I was stunned and scared and after I saw that he was bleeding we rushed him to the hospital. He was almost twenty feet away from me and I didn't even think for a second that the can would land near him. I was just trying to throw it at his feet. But it hit my brother in the head and it almost killed him.

The can was empty, not full, but it flew a long way and boy, it surprised both of us. I remember thinking right then I've got to watch my own strength. Really, I had that very thought. I recognized that if I got mad I could really hurt someone so I had better be careful. I was never really rough to anybody while sober, but I had no idea I was that strong. It was a lesson for me.

I was just getting into the Native games then and had no way of measuring my real strength, though I surprised myself one other time. This was kind of a strange thing. I found a big rock, a big boulder, down on the beach and I brought it to the Teen Center in town. I think this rock weighed between two-hundred-and-fifty and three-hundred pounds. It must have been a quarter mile that I carried it. Actually, I kind of dragged it up off the beach and when I got close to the Teen Center I lifted it up to my chest and carried it in.

People were really impressed with that. I was just bored at the time. You gotta be pretty bored to do something like that. It wasn't really anything special to me what I was doing, though. I didn't even feel I had exerted myself. I was just that strong then, a young buck.

When I brought the rock into the Teen Center, some guy was there who teased me about carrying around a big rock. I didn't like that. So I just placed it in the doorway and nobody in the Teen Center could move it. They all tried to lift it up, but nobody could do it. I thought it would be something to look at there. I don't know what happened to that boulder because I didn't lift it out. I think they took a hand truck and moved it out.

I've slimmed down over the years, to three-hundred-and-thirty pounds. I still need to weigh less than that. I don't even look like I weigh more than three hundred pounds because my bones are so big. I am never going to be a long distance runner, no matter what I do, but it would probably be better for my health if I was lighter.

From about five hundred pounds I got down to two-hundred-and-seventy-five in three months. I stopped eating sugar, salt and cooking oil. Pretty good diet, huh? And I started exercising, walk, walk, walk. When I got down to two-seventy-five nobody recognized me. I wasn't quite the Big Bob they knew anymore. I was only Pretty Big Bob.

I didn't get any shorter, though. I am the tallest one in my family. My father is only about five-foot-ten and my mother is average sized. But my father's dad Johnny was a tall man, well over six feet, I suppose. So I guess I get it from that side of the family. Going back even farther it would seem my size comes from the Irish whaler whom I never knew. My brothers aren't nearly so tall. I guess I got it all. There's only one Big Bob.

When I was growing up, I wasn't called Big Bob. The people at the World Eskimo-Indian Olympics in Fairbanks started calling me Big Bob later to differentiate me from the other Bobs who were around. My friends started it, just kidding around. I think it was another athlete, Greg Nothstine, who gave me the name after seeing me at the Games. That one's stuck by me. I don't mind since I'm actually the biggest Eskimo in the world, so I guess you can say that nickname is accurate. Could be one of my nephews, B.J., will be catching up to me soon. He's going to be big. He's not as tall, though. I took him to the Native Youth Olympics in Anchorage where high-school aged athletes compete in the games each spring, trying to get him started. But he got beat in some of the events and got frustrated. I told him the worst thing you can do is just give up.

I am proud of being the world's largest Eskimo.

I got that nickname more recently. Sometime in the 1980s, when I was already called Big Bob by everybody, I was appearing on a KBRW radio talk show in Barrow with the host, Earl Finkler, trying to raise money for the station. We were joking around, talking with Texas accents, being silly for probably about an-hour-and-a-half. We just got everybody laughing and they would call in with pledges for the station. And I just blurted out, "This is the biggest Eskimo in the world! Make a pledge right now to the world's biggest Eskimo!" And Earl said, "Yeah, and you'll sing for them, too." And all of a sudden people started calling in with pledge money, saying they'd give money, but only if I would sing. So I was requested to sing this country and western song called "Elvira."

After that, people started to think it was okay by me to call me the world's biggest Eskimo. I would guess they wouldn't say it unless they were sure it wouldn't offend me.

I kind of like it, actually. It's a real attention grabber. I go right up to tourists in Barrow and I know they're fresh off the boat, new in town, and I go right up to them and tell them they're looking at the biggest Eskimo in the world today. On the top of the world, too.

And I say it in Fairbanks at the World Eskimo-Indian Olympics. I break the ice that way. People are more attentive to what I say after I introduce myself this way. It gets their undivided attention.

A few years ago, after I retired from competition, I began going to WEIO as an official. One day I picked up the microphone to inform the audience and explain the history of our games. I found out if I started just talking about the background of the games, yabba, yabba, yabba, it might not get people's attention sitting in the stands at the Big Dipper Arena. But then I noticed if I could grab their attention in some way they'd start listening better and start getting into it.

One time I just said, "You're listening to the world's largest Eskimo." Using a real deep voice into the microphone. It was a technique I would use and it worked. Maybe they start thinking, "I'm listening to the world's biggest Eskimo." And they're listening to something interesting you say. They fall right into it and maybe after they're laughing, I go right into stories about the games. Then those people go away knowing that the games are really more than just games, but represent a way of life.

There might be 2,000 people at the Games on a Friday or Saturday night at the Big Dipper and if each crowd goes away with some knowledge you're educating a fair amount of people.

Sometimes I get asked how I know that I'm the world's largest Eskimo. But

I've been told that I am many times. I have never seen anyone bigger and I have never heard of anyone bigger. Taller, maybe, but not bigger. Eskimos tend to be built a lot smaller than me. Most of the Inupiat Eskimos are built low to the ground. No one has ever come up to me who was bigger and no one has ever told me he's met another Eskimo who is bigger.

I know there are bigger people out there. One time this buckskin preacher came up to me who was six-foot-nine and said he weighed four-hundred-and-twenty pounds. That was the first person I had to look up to literally. But he wasn't an Eskimo. And I'm a basketball fan, so I know that there are lots of professional basketball players in the National Basketball Association who are taller than me. But they're not Eskimos, either.

I am the world record-holder. If there is some Eskimo who is bigger, I would like to meet him. I'd ask him for his autograph. It is an interesting distinction to be known as the world's largest Eskimo and I don't mind it at all.

It draws attention to where I come from, too, and that's a good thing. Otherwise, people might never ask about where I live. It might never come up. They might not be curious. I like to talk to people and I like to educate people about Eskimos and the games in the World Eskimo-Indian Olympics, so anything that gets them talking with me is good.

One thing that I like about being big is that it has been something that draws kids to me. I didn't even realize it at first, but was told by one of the elders that kids gravitate to me. Once, when I was on television for the games, he noticed how kids all started yelling, "Big Bob's on TV! Big Bob's on TV!" He was really impressed with that, how the kids all knew me. He said those kids weren't even from Barrow.

This can be fun for me because even though I have quite a few nephews, I don't have any kids of my own and I like kids.

I know some kids are really frightened of me in the beginning. Little ones are scared, but when they hang around they start to like me. One little gal and her mom came up to me. The mother said to me, "Say hello to your friend." I said hi. They came up to me at work in Barrow and the mother said her daughter was always calling me her friend. And I didn't even know her. She was kind of shy and her mom put her on the spot. But kids do act friendly to me. They come up to me and hug me.

I am a very gentle person. I'm big, but I'm gentle and kids sense that. I would never yell at them or holler unless they were unruly. I guess I'm just a big teddy bear ready for a hug. I always give free hugs to little ones when they come up to me. Or sometimes I just pick them up off the floor. I am their friend. Little kids spend all of their time looking up at people and sometimes they like to touch the ceiling. I pick them up, hoist them in the air and I do it for them, put the ceiling within reach.

    They idolize famous people. I guess having kids who like you is one good benefit to being the world's largest Eskimo.

Chapter 7

One of the most amazing things about bowhead whales to us Eskimos is how old they get to be. We don't know exact ages since they obviously don't have birth certificates like people, but once in a while we get clues that the oldest whales might be as old as the oldest people.

A few years ago, a crew under the direction of my cousin, George Adams, who was the whaling captain, caught a whale believed to be more than one hundred years old. It was the fall whaling season and they hunted it off the shore near Point Barrow, just about a dozen miles out of town. The whales migrate past the Point in the spring and the fall.

The whale was average sized, about sixty-five feet long, and some of the bigger ones grow to about seventy-five feet, but when they brought it in, they found a flint harpoon head imbedded in the fat. And we stopped using those a century ago.

That would mean this whale survived a strike from a harpoon almost a hundred years earlier. How old was it then? It was a very old whale when it met George Adams.

Bowhead whales are magnificent creatures, so gigantic, and we follow regular cycles each year in our pursuit of them.

The first critical piece of equipment you need if you are going whaling is a good boat. We have longboats, fifteen or twenty feet in length, made out of driftwood, with the hulls then covered with bearded sealskin. Four or five skins are sewn together and stretched over the frame. It's stretched, then dried. Then we make sure there are no holes. Seal oil keeps the skin a little bit moist.

A wooden sled with runners is built separately from the boat. The boat is loaded on top of the sled and is dragged out onto the ice. Then it is pulled along the ice until an open lead is reached.

But before you reach that point, there's a lot of work to be done.

In the early spring, the whaling captain takes note of the improvement in the weather and he senses from the changes in the air that there will be openings in the ice. When the crew captain feels this, you know that whaling season is around the corner.

The hunt for whales actually begins in late April or early May, depending on the weather and if the sea ice is beginning to move out. Once in a great while we can go out as early as April, but definitely by May.

Before we go out the captain calls the crew together, mostly family members. He starts issuing orders and plans for everyone to get ready, to haul out the equipment and begin re-stretching the rope we use on the harpoons. There is a lot of rope involved in whaling, a lot of rope. There are also snowmachines to tune up, sleds to repair, and cutting equipment to sharpen, including ulus, our traditional knife.

There is no official date that we start. It is up to the whaling captain, but it will be about a month from the time he meets with the crew until the start of the season. A whole month of serious preparation is needed, at a minimum. There is a lot to do, so I'd say that you are definitely getting ready by the early part of April. Once the equipment is checked and cleaned comes the hard part.

The whaling captain assembles his crew and they meet with the other whaling captains and crews and all the men are combined into teams. They start building trails through the snow and ice, over the pressure ridges and the rough ice. Sometimes you only have to go out a mile from shore. Other times, it's many miles. It varies.

At that time of year the area is totally covered with snow and ice. The ice that moved back and forth during the winter really tears up the surface, so pressure ridges bulge up. They get really big. Just to make the trail smooth you have go out before any equipment is moved. We use ice picks and shovels and anything you can use to chop ice in order to knock down big ice blocks.

This ice trail is for snowmachines and to haul the boats through, plus all the people and gear being carried, the food we will need to set up camp. We need to bring enough food to last one or two months.

The beginning spot in the whaling season is pretty much where the whaling captain chooses. It's totally up to him. A lot of times it will be where the last whale was caught at the end of the last season. We trust the judgment of the whaling captain. He knows best. It's his call.

It's a tremendous amount of work to clear the snow and ice. There's so much snow on top of everything and it's all frozen. The big pressure ridges that you've got to go over might be one or two stories high. You've got to remove the ice blocks. And it's those you've got to watch out for because part of the equipment you're bringing through is explosives.

Whaling has definitely changed over the years from when our ancestors had those flint-tipped harpoons. Our harpoons carry an explosive charge. When you shoot a dart into the whale, it's loaded with black powder. When it collides with a bone, it sets off a fuse. That ignites the black powder and explodes inside the whale.

It's a big bang, all right. That's what we're aiming to do, get an instant kill, so that the whale shouldn't have to suffer.

A direct hit for an instant kill would be right on the vertebrae. That would immobilize the whale and soon it will die and turn over. These whales weigh sixty, seventy or eighty tons. We don't know exactly how much each whale weighs. Where are you going to get the scale? But they definitely are the biggest animals on earth. What we do is measure a foot square and multiply it times the length. Pretty good guess, huh?

Whaling captains get a lot of respect in the community. They are in positions of authority and what they do benefits the whole community. Whaling captains inherit their jobs so the position will be in the family for generations.

My grandfather Vincent Nageak was a whaling captain. His equipment was so old. He had a brass type of dart gun that was more than a hundred years old. It's an antique that he was using. But the harpoons — the harpooning dart guns — were modified and improved so the bomb that goes into the whale is accurate and kills immediately.

Using updated equipment absolutely makes hunting whales safer for the men. It cuts down on the struggle with the whale. In the old days they only used harpoons and lances. In order to kill the whale, you'd have to be on top of it in the water. The men would have to drive the long harpoon inside trying to find the heart or the vertebrae. Your boat would be right next to the whale while it was thrashing around. Men would climb on top of the whale's back. The water would be splashing around and practically sinking the boat. I've seen men go in the water up to their neck still trying to find the right spot as a whale started to submerge. That was something to see. The man was trying not to drown and trying to find the right place to plunge his harpoon in and the boat was trying to stay afloat. Pretty dramatic. You could get hurt that way.

I can't remember how old I was when I first realized what the significance of hunting whales is to Inupiat people. It was always going on around me. I sensed the excitement in the air when the preparations were being made. I think I was nine years old when I saw that old man dance for joy when a whale was landed.

As a youngster I was first impressed with just how big this animal was and I wondered, How the heck did they kill it? The first whale I saw was dead and the people were just preparing to pull it up out of the sea onto the ice. Bowhead whales are basically black and the blubber, the fat of the whale, is pink when it is butchered.

I was out at the whaling camp when they dragged it out of the water to butcher it. It was cut up and then all the meat and muktuk was brought by sled dog team into town. Everything except the skeleton was carried in. They leave the bones out there. The rib cage looks like a stripped-down shell. That's all that would be left out there in the ice. Late at night, the polar bears come in and feed on the remains when they get hungry. They scavenge any little bit of meat left on the carcass.

I was in awe of the size of the whale. It was the biggest animal I had ever seen in my life. I was impressed. I had been eating muktuk my whole life and wondered where it came from and then I saw.

The whale was harpooned and the boats towed it up to the ice. They used a short strap attached between the whale and a boat and then a long tow rope. All the boats tied themselves to this longer rope and the crews paddled in. The whale was brought in by human power, the strength of the men who killed it.

The crews are made up of the best men in the community, tough men, and they are hand-picked, selected by each crew captain. Mostly, each crew is made up of individual family members, brothers, nephews and cousins. Generally, you can only fit eight or nine men in a boat, eight rowers and one sitting in the rear to steer. That was the most important spot.

Whale hunting is not like fishing where you might move around looking for where the fish are biting all the time. It's not like hunting with a rifle, either. If you are hunting caribou, you go out across the land until you catch up with the herd. You pretty much are looking for only one whale. Actually, it's not that you are searching for one as much as waiting for one to come to you. We only go after whales that come near the ice, close to shore. We don't search the whole ocean until we find one. When you know one is close enough, you go after it. You don't go out there and just sit and wait. You bide your time at the camp waiting for one to get close enough.

Whales are important to us for many reasons. Everything we need to survive in the cold winter months is contained in the whale. Everything that the whale provides we need. The minerals and vitamins the blubber contains. The oil, everything. This body we have needs some kind of protection from the elements.

The food we eat gives us this protection, too. The blood and the oil that goes through the whale's body gives us the protein in the meat that sustains us through the winter.

My grandfather was a whaling captain for a long time, then he gave the equipment to my father, Robert Aiken. He was a whaling captain for about fifteen years, but couldn't afford to go year after year, so he gave it back. He gave up the job and turned the equipment over to my uncle, Roy Nageak.

By the time my father inherited the whaling captainship, I was grown and was working full-time. I was too busy in my career and the world, so I never went out with him. I just worked and provided for us in other ways.

My chance to go whaling the first time came when I was much younger. I was about fourteen when my grandfather invited me to go out. I was excited. At that time, outboard motors were just starting to become popular, so we hardly ever rowed anywhere. Only when we got close to a whale and had to be quiet. We shut off the engine and paddled. We would row up close to get a good shot with the harpoon, trying not to spook the whale.

It was very special when I was told I would be able to go out whaling for the first time. Being asked to go meant something. Up until then I was too young, so being asked meant my grandfather felt I was ready, that I was becoming a man. I was not given much advance notice or time to think about it. One day they just told me they wanted me to come along and take a spot along with the crew. I just jumped right in. Right then and there.

I was very scared of the ice floes at first as the boat slipped in-between them. They towered over us. I thought the wind would move them in and crush us. I was scared, but I knew if I showed fear it was all over. The harpooner was telling me that the crew didn't need anyone along out there who is scared of the water or scared of the ice. That could hurt the crew. It would mean bad luck.

He was also telling me they didn't allow for any mistakes in the boat when they went out. It was cold and it was a long day and there was a chance a whale would come along and you would have to work fast and help kill the whale and bring it in. There was a lot of responsibility. There was no room for anybody who would slow them down, or who was lacking because of fear.

I felt there was a lot of pressure on me to behave a certain way and to perform. But it also meant that I knew the rules. They were clear. You can't screw up. It was clear a lot was riding on every man. If you can't demonstrate to your whaling captain, and to your relatives, that you can take it and you can earn your keep, you're outta there.

It was obvious that they wanted to test me out and see if I was ready to be a man and be a whale hunter. At that time I had not yet participated in the Games, so I didn't know as much about my strength or about myself. We never got a whale that first time, never even saw one.

There are thirty-five or forty crews who go out hunting for whales from Barrow alone and the Alaska Eskimo Whaling Commission has a quota of forty-five strikes a year granted by the International Whaling Commission for us Eskimos. Barrow's share in recent years was twenty-two strikes. A strike doesn't mean a catch, it means a hit. If a whale gets hit by a harpoon and you don't bring it in it still counts as one of your strikes. That whale might be wounded and die later and since people think whales are pretty rare, they don't want too many of them to be hunted. I have some strong feelings about that. I don't think they know what they're talking about. Some people who don't know much about it would prefer Eskimos never hunted whales again. They'd rather have us all sit home and weave baskets. But the whales help keep us alive.

In any case, not every crew gets a whale every season. We cooperate and share with each other because that happens and because whales are so big there is enough for everybody.

There is instruction early on about what makes a good whale hunter. Before we're old enough to go out as part of a crew, we might participate in the butchering of the whale or transporting it back to town. We are told at a young age to get in on it. We are told to stay alert and watch what other crews are doing. We are taught every little thing that could mess up a successful strike.

When a whale comes near your camp, other crews pass the word that it is coming your way. Then you prepare yourself mentally and physically. You think about where you're going to strike that whale, what part of the body you're going to hit. As the harpooner you are thinking of these things and visualizing what you're going to do before you even see the whale.

You can't see the whale until it surfaces to breathe. You look at it to see how big it is and that gives you an idea where the vertebrae are and where to strike. Until you see the whale and see its size, you can't determine where the perfect strike is. The hunter will either be going for the vertebrae in the back, or going for the heart.

From the blow hole, on top, where a whale spouts, there is a bone that runs straight back to the tail. Either you aim for that on top about four feet behind the blowhole, or you aim for the heart. The heart is below the water line, also about four feet back from the blow hole, and when you strike below the water line, you'd better make sure it's going straight in. That's a harder target to hit. The blow hole is critical. It's the measuring place to be able to mark either one of your spots.

One time when I was young and out whaling I saw hundreds and hundreds of whales passing by. Bowheads, right whales, gray whales, belugas. You felt pretty small out there. You could see whales jumping, coming right out of the water with their whole bodies, these big monsters. Each time they'd make a big splash. Not just one whale, but twenty of them coming out of the water. That was something I'll never forget.

Hunting for bowheads can be very dangerous. I have heard about a few boats being tipped over by whales, but I never saw it with my own eyes. It definitely has happened. It's not just a myth.

A story I heard was that a few boats were around one whale when the whale was harpooned. One boat was in the wrong place, going in the wrong direction after being told to stay away from that side of the whale. It startled the whale and the whale flipped the boat over with its tail. It didn't knock them sideways, it knocked them longways. The boat was turned over and there were two guys missing. They just disappeared in the deep, deep water.

The current is very strong down there, the undertow is tremendous. This was years ago it happened, but that's not the only time I heard of that kind of disaster.

Another incident happened a few years ago when people were pulling a whale up on top of the ice. The pulley they were using snapped, the ice broke, and the pulley hit a couple of women and one was killed. The wooden block and tackle hit them. I guess that shows that even after a whale is dead it can still be dangerous.

Once a whale is towed out of open water, it is pulled up onto solid ice. The spot must be carefully picked so the ice won't collapse or break through. Unlike most hunting or fishing, you can't just load the catch on a snowmachine or a dog sled and take it home. The whale is so huge you can't take it anywhere else once you run out of water. Everyone comes out and pulls on the block and tackle to pull the whale onto the ice. It's a tug of war right on top of the ice.

There might be a hundred-and-fifty people involved trying to move that whale. The whole town comes out. I've pulled many times helping out. It's amazing how much muscle it takes to move the dead weight of the whale.

Pulling a whale is like trying to move one of those big, old black railroad engines across the road. Everybody is pulling with all their might. Your hands get raw, your muscles strain, and you look down and you've moved the whale one inch. You do that over and over again. At first, you're only trying to move the head out of the water so you can start butchering. And all in all you're only moving it the length of the whale. Fifty, sixty feet. It's not like you're trying to move it five miles.

But the whale weighs sixty tons, 120,000 pounds, or more. That's a lot of effort. It's incredible to think of. Everybody helps. There's nobody sitting around. The same is true when the butchering starts. There's enough work to keep everybody busy.

Once the butchering begins I have a hook and a rope in my hands. I go along next to the people who are cutting up the whale. With my meat hook, I am pulling off the slabs they cut and putting them off to the side, then moving the chunks of muktuk to a certain area. Then they get cut up into smaller pieces.

There are a lot of procedures involved in cutting up the whale. The belt part, the part around the mid-section, belongs to the whaling captain and his crew. They share it with the people who helped tow the whale with their boats, all the crews and whaling captains who were out there hunting. The tail section goes to the crew, too. The rest of the mid-section would be for the community and so is the front part, from the middle up to the head area. The head and the flippers go to the whaling captain. The baleen is divided up between the whaling captains and crew.

The baleen is what the whales use to eat instead of teeth. It is made out of a substance that is like horns on other mammals, or fingernails on people. They are fringed with very thin, very fine pieces of what looks like hair hanging from the upper jaw. A bowhead whale has about six hundred of them. The hair-like stuff strains the plankton. These whales eat a lot of shrimp and things like that off the ocean floor or the ocean surface.

When you have a lot of people involved and you have good help, it still takes eight or more hours to butcher the whale. But if a whale is very big and there aren't quite enough people working, it can take three or four days to cut it up. There was one we got in Barrow in the spring of 1995, taken by Arnold Brower and his crew, which was sixty-eight feet. It was really heavy.

Once a whale is captured and butchered and the meat is taken into town and stored in the ice cellar, if the whaling captain feels he should go back out, then he and his crew go back out. In the old days, the crew would stay out until they got three or four whales. But they butchered whales a lot faster, too.

The killing of a whale is a great thing for a community. As soon as the hunters catch it, it's time for a celebration. That very day. When a crew lands a whale, as soon as it can put somebody ashore someone is sent, a son or a nephew, by snow-machine into the village to tell everybody. The messenger carries a flag with him and flies it. It's the family flag with a special design that's been passed on for generations.

They bring the flag home and run it up on top of the house, telling everybody the family got a whale. That announces they would like everyone to come help butcher it and pull it in.

After the whale is butchered they'll be boiling it and cooking the muktuk and holding a celebration party. They'll do that when the captains come home, or even right out on the ice. The muktuk is the tastiest part of the whale. The muktuk is the blubber, or skin, taken from the upper epidermis of the whale. It has a fishy taste, it's a little bit oily, but when it's soft, it melts in your mouth.

Muktuk contains minerals that are anti-freeze for the Eskimo body. It tastes fishy, but not like biting into fish. I can't really describe it because it has a taste all unto itself.

It's too fresh to eat raw. It will bloat you. It's better to boil it and salt it. Sometimes people get so excited that we got a whale that there's a temptation to dig right in and eat too much of it. They look forward to having whale meat for the whole year so they can't wait to taste it. It becomes a big community event right there on the ice, with everyone making soup, sandwiches and munching muktuk while butchering.

The women want the men to see the fruits of their labor right away while they are still working so they might be cooking up a storm even as the men are still butchering. The whole community will rush down to have a taste. It's a community effort to bring the whale in and it's a community sharing in the whale itself.

Even when everyone's back home, anyone who walks in the door gets a share. After the initial celebration, a lot of the meat is stored in the ice cellar. Then you wait a few months, until late June or early July, when the whaling is done, and you have a big festival. A week before the celebration, people start cutting up the chunks of meat into smaller pieces that can be carried home in little storage bags. And at the whaling festivals, the crew walks around with buckets of muktuk and gives it away to families.

That's just part of the additional sharing. It's a big party for the town. People take off from work at mid-day. Everything in town stops. Women make duck soup, smoked salmon, chowder and caribou stew and all kinds of soups. It's just a festive occasion.

This is one party that is linked directly to catching a whale. There would be no festival if no one caught a whale that year. I remember there was one year nobody got a whale and there was no festival. The people were upset! I don't think they talked about it much, but it weighed on everybody's mind. It's not something that happens very often, but you have to remember, we live with the elements. Sometimes these elements don't cooperate the way you would like. Most of the time they cooperate, or you work to make them cooperate.

The whales were going through, they hadn't disappeared, but we didn't get them. The ice kept blowing in and out so it was constantly blocking the boats. When the sea ice is doing that we can't get our boats through, so we couldn't approach the whales even though we knew they were out there. It's not safe to go out when it's like that. We have black powder bombs in the boats and we can't afford to risk crashing into the ice. It's too sensitive.

No whales for Barrow that year. I wouldn't want to go through another year like that.

Chapter 8

The bowhead whale is one of the most important things in the world to the Inupiat Eskimos of Barrow. In a way it symbolizes everything about us. The whale feeds us, nurtures us, and defines our culture.

Whaling is one of the most important activities of our life. Everyone is excited when the hunters go out on the sea ice and catch a whale. The word is spread that they are towing back a whale and everyone goes to the beach to participate in cutting it up. That's why the whale meat and muktuk is shared with everyone in town, because everyone helps do something to bring it in.

Growing up in Barrow we were exposed to whaling at an early age. It's part of the life there. No one has to tell you that hunting for whales is a big thing. You can tell. It just became fixed in our minds how important it was, even if we weren't old enough to hunt yet. When I was a kid my grandfather was a whaling captain. That meant he got to choose his own crew and to direct one of the skinboats on the ocean as they pursued whales.

It took a real man to go out on the water and we knew chasing whales was very dangerous. Little kids didn't get to go along. You had to be mature, grown up, strong, before your father or grandfather asked you to go. And if you were invited into a boat it meant that you were considered in training to be a man. It was a sign that you were respected by the whaling captain. If you weren't old enough or experienced enough to handle yourself out there on the ice, you wouldn't be allowed to come along.

I was in my teens when the elders said to my granddad, "Why don't you bring him along?"

Whales were important to Inupiat Eskimos, providing us with meat and muktuk. But that did not represent our complete diet. There were no big grocery stores in Barrow carrying fresh meat in the 1950s and 1960s. All families hunted and fished to feed themselves. The Inupiat people have had a subsistence culture, living off the land, for thousands of years. It is at the root of our existence.

My grandfather was the family leader in whaling, but my father Robert was a big provider. He did a lot of hunting for caribou with my uncles and we kids were eventually included in those hunts in a season that ran from the spring until fall.

It might be compared to a family business in the other states, where a family owned a small store and let the kids work there. Or a family farm where everyone worked. You get educated by doing what is important to your family. They break you in gradually.

Sometimes the caribou herd trotted right up near town, would just be a few miles away on the outskirts of the homes. But other times we would take the dog team and mush inland to hunt, and later, the snowmachine. We would stay out until we got four or five big bulls. On one big caribou hunt my father and uncles would get fifteen hundred pounds of meat. Only men were allowed to go hunting in the old days. Later we began hunting ducks and geese. I don't really remember us hunting for them until I was high school age.

From the first time I tasted caribou meat I loved it. It was so good. I think it's the best meat in the world. It's better than T-bone steak, better than roast beef. Juicier. I remember once in a while we had steak at school for lunch and it was supposed to be the biggest treat. But I didn't like it as much as caribou meat. That was the taste I grew up with.

When you are young you just eat everything your parents give you. I didn't even recognize what I was eating at first. Only later, once I began to hunt for caribou, did I realize this is what I've been eating all these years.

Caribou resemble deer and elk, which we don't ever see in Barrow, but I know are common in the lower states. Caribou have antlers and the same general build as those animals. They're not as big as moose, but a good-sized caribou might weigh five hundred pounds. By the time you got done butchering them and trimming the bone you still had enough meat to last a long time.

Too long to leave lying around the house without it spoiling. Eskimos have been hunting caribou for a lot longer time than we've had refrigeration, so techniques were developed over the years to store the meat and to take advantage of the area where we live. Before we had electricity, people had to be clever.

Once we hauled the meat home we would store it in an ice cellar that my dad built, or at my grandpa's. The land in and around Barrow is permafrost. Two feet under the top layer of soil the ground stays permanently frozen, even in the warmest days of summer.

What hunters learned to do was to dig ten-to-twenty feet deep and make a storage space. We'd cut through the dirt, dig through the permafrost, and then create a chamber underneath. We'd make a tunnel in the earth and at the bottom of that tunnel we enlarged the perimeter. We would throw down fresh snow to make a floor and that would keep the chamber and the meat dirt-free. The snow would preserve the flavor of the meat.

We could keep the meat down there for up to ten years. It would still be good. It would stay frozen. This was our walk-in freezer. We didn't need electricity for that when we had the elements working for us.

The tunnel was the key to the convenience. The chest wasn't outright buried by itself in the snow or ground. With the tunnel for access, we could go down there any time we got hungry for a taste of caribou. If you built a good tunnel, you had an ice cellar that would last.

It was permanent, just like the permafrost. Those cellars and storage areas were built to last under the ice, twenty years, thirty years, even longer. Some of them are much older than me. I kid you not. There are some really old ice cellars in Barrow.

I went caribou hunting myself for the first time right after high school. I was about eighteen years old. I was not a very good shot when I started out, but I got a caribou every once in a while.

I was very proud when I got my first caribou because it meant I was providing. It meant my parents could eat fresh meat that I killed. All those years they had been providing me with the food. It felt good to harvest a caribou, but even better to provide. That made me a contributing member of the society.

My family was on a trip inland, about sixty miles southeast of Barrow towards the Colville and Kuparuk Rivers. That's in the general direction of Prudhoe Bay, where the oil field is and the beginning of the Alaska Pipeline. We were going to build a cabin on the Kuparuk River. As we went along, there were caribou following me. I looked back and saw one about fifty yards back and thought, "Hmm, that caribou looks good out there." I figured if he wants to follow me, I might as well pick him off. So I took out my rifle and took a shot. I got it in one shot, gutted it, and took it home.

Ordinarily, in past days, I would have become a hunter at a younger age than that. But I grew up in the era when kids were still sent away from home to attend high school far away. The villages didn't have their own schools and the only way we could get a formal education was going outside our home area. That meant I had missed out on learning a lot of the subsistence hunting techniques because I was forced to go to school elsewhere. So when I got my first caribou I was still learning that the right time of year to hunt was the spring and that the time to stay away from caribou is when they're rutting. After rutting season, caribou make for sweet meat.

When my parents saw that I had killed my first caribou they were pleased. Then dad taught me the best time of year to harvest them. That was the true beginning of my hunting career, and over the last twenty-five years or so I have also hunted for walrus and ugruk, geese and ducks.

The cabin was built on the river for a good reason. That's where the fish are. My family set up a fish camp as a base to go after grayling, trout and whitefish and they spent most of the fall outside of Barrow stockpiling fish for the winter.

I love to eat fish. Whitefish and every kind of salmon. King salmon, red salmon, silver salmon.

Most of the time I was in school, so I didn't get to go fishing, but fish was a major part of our diet. Before they built the cabin my parents would camp. They'd bring a tent, stove, sleeping bags and set up by the river in the fall.

Although most of the fishing was done after freeze up, even afterwards, when the rivers were frozen over with a coating of ice, they kept up the fishing for a little while. They'd drop a line through a hole and go ice fishing. They could still catch grayling and trout and ling cod.

The Aiken family also catches salmon with nets at Elson Lagoon, right out at Point Barrow, a few miles from downtown. We set out gill nets and mainly get salmon, but that's not all. We've caught seals that way. And once, a few years ago, we caught a porpoise. Way up north here. Everybody was surprised at that. A lot of other people from town got porpoises that year. Mom cooked the porpoise and cut it up like muktuk, treated it just like the skin and blubber that comes from a whale.

The meat was good, salty like seal. She fried it. Yum. It was something else. Different. At first I only took a nibble, but after a while it started tasting really good. That was a rarity, though, the only time I had porpoise meat.

Whale, seal, caribou, geese and ducks were on our table much more often.

Geese don't come that close to town. We hunt for geese at the cabin out by the river. We live at the cabin for a time and the geese migrate our way. There is only about a two-week window of opportunity where we can hunt them in the spring. One hunting trip we harvested one-hundred-and-fifty of them. That may seem like an enormous number of geese, but there are a lot of mouths to feed in our family and that food has to last quite a long time.

The sky was just filled with geese. I mean really filled. We were traveling by snowmachine and we startled the geese. A black cloud rose up from one of the lakes and it was nothing but solid geese. They darkened the sky. Thousands and thousands of geese just coming back north. I was in total awe. I didn't think there were that many geese in the whole world.

I have heard some people say that the geese might be getting extinct. Extinct my foot! I think there are more geese than there are people in this world.

Other times we'd hunt king eider ducks. We'd go along the coast outside Barrow to the west. That's the opposite way from where we go for geese. There was a certain spot we'd pick along the cliffs where the ducks would fly right overhead. If you didn't know where to go you couldn't hunt them. But if you knew where they were coming, you were all right. In a single day in the spring we would get between thirty and fifty ducks. And they would last us all summer.

Most of our hunting would take place at that time of year. After the ducks and the geese get to Barrow they're ready to lay their eggs. We stop then and let them grow their young. The rest of our hunting we do in the fall when we are storing up for the winter.

The pattern of hunting is very simple. The animals are on the move, migrating, twice a year. They are leaving winter homes for summer homes, or leaving summer homes for winter homes. And the people are getting ready for the change of the seasons.

Chapter 9

Nearly fifteen years ago, the International Whaling Commission wanted to stop us from whaling altogether and we started something called "The Tundra Rebellion." They were trying to convince us whales were going extinct and we proved them wrong.

We were ready and could easily have taken up arms. But we got our heads together and thought we could beat those guys a different way. Just by talking to them we thought we might be able to convince them we knew something about whales. And we did it. We pulled it off.

The International Whaling Commission wanted to ban whaling completely and they were acting long distance. We see things in the north that they never see. They were acting from hearsay and that's really upsetting to us. We are out on the ice. We see the countless whales. We know they are there. Nobody in the world knows more about bowhead whales than Inupiat Eskimos of the North Slope of Alaska.

Others who never even come to the Arctic can't know the things about whales that Eskimos do. We had town meetings, radio programs and the politicians in town all got together and started working on this to lobby for us. They got their heads together and fought back with their wisdom.

We thought we might challenge them about some of the oil company activity in the region. We tried to take their focus off the whales.

The whaling commission does set quotas that we have to abide by, but we still get our share of strikes. We still get our opportunities to go after the whales that we need for our community.

The rules about whaling have changed as much as our own whaling has changed. We used to be able to do what we wanted and what we thought was best. But whaling has grown more sophisticated.

You can't be hanging on the rope with the whale dragging you all over the Arctic Ocean. In the old days, whaling was harder. Some of the whalers from Ireland and all those other worlds, came over to our territory and they had bigger ships and more advanced technology. We learned things from them. But they were commercial whalers. They were only interested in harvesting as many whales as they could. They wanted the baleen and they wanted the oil, but not for themselves, just to sell. Our whaling has always been for subsistence.

That was a hard thing to convince the International Whaling Commission about. They thought we were commercial whalers. They considered us to be whalers who were businessmen. It took a lot of talking for us to convince them that we were just trying to survive out there.

What the whaling commission did that really disgusted us was try to make a deal with us, saying, "If you give up whaling, we will send you all this beef." What an insult.

Beef from cows. That was crazy. That showed they didn't understand us at all. They were disregarding our history, our culture and our traditions. It was an insult and didn't make any sense to us at all. To eat beef up north in Barrow after so many generations of living off the animals we are used to, of depending on the whale meat, we'd freeze. We get certain vitamins and minerals from the way we eat. Beef would not sustain us through the winter.

They were just trying to impose their way of life on Eskimos. We didn't want to have anything to do with that. It would have been a sad day. Kind of ridiculous for them to think of a trade like that. They were being foolish to suggest such a thing.

I feel the same way about those "Save the Whales" people in the lower forty-eight states. And animal rights activists, too. I cannot even remotely identify with what they are saying and trying to do. Not at all. We have lived this way for thousands of years and don't want to change. What gives them the right to try to change us?

We have dealt with all of those kind of people before. They have come to Barrow. They came to try to stop us from hunting the whales. We didn't rebuke them or anything, but we just showed them exactly what we were doing and how it related to our history and ancestors. Some of them saw what we were doing and respected us and stopped trying to get us to give up hunting whales. Animal rights activists? What's that? Animals don't have rights. Man, I don't know where they get this thinking from. I think it's just focusing on the wrong things. The only way to survive up north is to eat the animals who also live here.

I can understand why there was some protest going about commercial whaling. Commercial whalers exploited the bowheads. They just took the blubber or the baleen and left everything else. We didn't waste like that. We wouldn't waste any part of the whale. The main reason the old commercial whalers wanted baleen was so they could be used in the making of girdles. So the women in the rest of the country could look skinny. Garter belts and girdles. Corsets. For the old whalers, whaling was a job, a profession. For us it's a way of life, the way we survive. Two different things.

It might just be that people who live in the 1990s have trouble understanding that there are still Eskimos and other people who live off the land. There once was a time when everyone in the United States lived off the land. They forget that. But they might think that time is gone for everyone when it's not.

Just because some people who live in the cities are vegetarians, they think everyone should be, that no one should live off the animals on the land anymore because they don't.

You see all of these people in India and they are starving. At the same time they have animals all around them and they won't eat them. To them cows are sacred. I can understand that they do it for religious reasons, but I think the people in this country who adopted that idea of not eating meat got the idea that animals have rights. That's silly.

Even if it's for religious reasons, I can't identify with people who worship animals. Animals sacred? Worship them? Worse than that, I can't understand that people would rather starve to death than eat the animals. To me, that's foolishness. It's foolish for me to think I could ever worship a whale. If we did that, we'd all die.

There is a difference between worshipping whales and respecting whales. Inupiat Eskimos have a lot of respect for whales. Remember, they give us so much of what we need. We are not up here in Barrow sport hunting or fishing for trophies. We are trying to stay alive. That's all we're trying to do. There's a difference between survival and sport.

I don't care much for the arguments of people who say we don't need the whale anymore because we have a grocery store in Barrow now. The store is a good place and I like to eat a lot of the things they have. But most of my life I ate food from the wild, frozen fish, frozen caribou dipped in seal oil. This is what I grew up with and what I'm used to.

By eating this way we stay healthy. The Eskimos of old survived the harshest winters. They had energy and all the minerals stored up inside their bodies and that gave them the strength to endure the cold weather. You just wouldn't be an Eskimo if you didn't eat that way. You see some Eskimos moving south to Anchorage. I don't know how they do it. That's not the way I want to live my life.

Hunting for whales is a subsistence activity, but the act itself is important to us. The value it has for our culture is part of being alive in Barrow. Our ancestors in the old days didn't only share the whales they got, but everything else. If somebody caught a seal, all the neighbors would come by and get a piece of the seal. It was sharing among whole extended families and the whole community. Those hunters were providers who went out hunting for their families and for all families besides their own.

This was part of the communal outlook that it was man against the elements, that we had to work together and combine our forces, or we could be defeated by the snow and ice. This is a harsh place and we have to help each other when we can.

This land is so vast it makes you feel small. Nature can do that in many ways, no matter how big you are and there aren't any Eskimos bigger than me.

Once I was driving along in my truck in another part of Alaska with my family and we saw this huge mountain right beside the road. I couldn't help but be so humbled by it that I stopped the truck, got out and looked straight up at this mountain. I thought, How could a rock be this big? That humbling spirit is the same humbleness we feel towards our relationship between ourselves and the elements.

It is something much bigger than yourself. The elements are so impressive they can create a humbling spirit and make people want to look out for each other. It goes back a long time. The relatives who started traveling together in the wintertime started it. They took care of things together. They hunted together, foraged for food together, shared together.

I like to think they solved their problems together, maybe better than we do today. I try to look at sharing the same way now, but I don't necessarily think it was better to live in a different time. I'm satisfied with living now.

Chapter 10

The trick to hunting ugruk, the bearded seal, is to shoot them just in the right spot of their bodies, when they're laying in just the right spot on the ice, so they won't fall in the water and be lost.

I have several rifles that I keep locked up in my room at home, and they all have different power. But they are all built for long-range shooting, with a telescope on them.

In late spring, seals get out on top of the ice and lie there in the sun and you can see them from shore. We drive out along the road near Barrow and park our vehicles, then take aim. You aim below the neck, or right below the head. And that's the spot you must hit. You aim for an instant kill. You have to. If you hit a seal on the ice and you just wound it, then the seal will slip into the water and get away. Even if you hit it and the bullet doesn't have an instant effect, the seal might fall into the water. It may die, but you won't get the meat.

It takes patience and skill to be a good hunter. As well as practice and a lot of knowledge. Not only about how to hunt, but knowledge of the elements and the water's currents and knowledge of preparedness. Everything. You just don't go out on the ice shooting off a weapon with no background or training.

The seals are pretty close to land, maybe a hundred yards at the closest. They make breathing holes when the snow and ice starts melting and they usually dig and claw their way to the surface. Or sometimes there are already cracks in the ice and they pull themselves up and sunbathe. They can lie out there for hours. They can sense man at quite a distance if the wind is blowing in the wrong direction, so we have to be careful if we try to approach for a closer shot. Just the slightest noise will get their attention. They can just dive in the water so fast and you never see them again.

A perfect shot will leave the seal flat on the ice within reach. Even then getting to the seal can be a challenge. If the ice is breaking up, as it usually is then, it can easily crack open under your feet. If you are reckless you can find yourself in the cold water and you'll be in trouble quick.

In the World Eskimo-Indian Olympics we have a game where competitors leap out and touch a wooden stick with their feet. It's called the toe kick and it simulates the manner in which you must jump from ice floe to ice floe when hunting. You need balance and an ability to jump a certain distance. It has a very practical application when you are going after natchiq seals.

Natchiq seals, or ringed seals, weigh between seventy and one hundred pounds, compared to ugruks, which weigh a minimum of five hundred pounds and can be much bigger than that. They are big animals and it's not easy to just pick one up and throw it over your shoulder. Not even I can do that and I'm pretty strong. We use ulus, the cutting tools Inupiat people have used for centuries. They have sharp, half-moon shaped blades and wood handles. You really can do a good job with an ulu. Actually, if you are planning to travel a long distance after you shoot seal, the first thing you do is cut out some of the intestines. That is the first thing that spoils. Then you take the seal home and the women skin it and do the rest of the butchering.

The goal is to get as many ugruk seals as you can at once because there is a small window of opportunity. It might only be three weeks out of the entire year when you can hunt them. I'd be lucky to get five or six in a season.

Oh, man, it takes a lot of time and effort to get a seal. I'd go out early in the morning and come back late at night or in the wee hours of the morning and I might get one. If I was very lucky, I'd get more than one at a time. But that would be a very lucky day.

There are two kinds of seals that are hunted near Barrow. The ringed seal is smaller, about the length of a dog, though heavier. We don't eat them very much. The bearded seal is much more important to us.

We use the skin of the bearded seal to cover the frames of our umiaqs, the same boats we use for hunting whales. The skin is very durable and when it is in the water it doesn't drag or make noise like aluminum boats do. Aluminum makes a startling noise. When a skinboat hits an iceberg, the sound is a very low thud. When an aluminum boat hits ice, it makes a very loud, clanging noise in the water. And away goes whatever you're hunting for. The skinboats are better for approaching whales, but when the season is ending and the ice is really thawing out, people use their aluminum boats. They are a lot faster and more efficient. And the whales may be traveling much faster in open water. They might dive at a greater distance from you.

Just about all parts of the ugruk are edible. I like to eat seal meat boiled or roasted. My mom roasts seal with potatoes and carrots and onions. It's like a stew and it's delicious. It's like steaming the seal. Umm, good. When a seal is cut up and cooked in this way it looks exactly like beef, but it tastes fishy. There are a lot of minerals and vitamins. The liver is very rich in vitamins. Very tasty.

We have sun-dried seal meat from bearded seal. When it is dried out we cut it into sections. Seal oil, the fat, is a preservative. We cut the fat into strips first and all the juices run out. I don't know what to compare it to that people eat in the rest of the United States. I'm sure it would take them some time to get used to the fishy taste. Of course, everything from the ocean tastes fishy.

Seals are not the hardest of animals to hunt. In the old days, before we had high-powered rifles, we used nets. We would poke holes in the ice and set a trap for passing seals. We'd stretch out the net and they'd get caught when they were swimming by. They'd get curious and get all tangled up. Sometimes you could catch five or six seals at a time. Actually, once in a while we still do that with nets, but it's more common to hunt them one at a time with rifles. Sea mammals are an important part of our diet.

So are walrus. People of Barrow don't seem to know when walrus are going to come every summer. When they do come, walrus generally come as close to shore as seals. I have been hunting for walrus since I was young, with my dad, or my cousins.

The prized delicacy of a walrus is the flipper. The elders especially like the flipper that is full of protein. They love that stuff. But to tell you the truth, one flipper can stink up the whole house. It has the odor of decay. It's really a strong smell. And you can't eat very much of it at one time, either. It's very rich and if you eat too much you get high and sleepy.

Just as if you took some kind of drug, you can get high on walrus flipper. Most people won't understand that, they can't identify with it at all. But really, you can get a buzz.

There are some things you can't eat at all after you eat walrus flipper. You cannot eat canned fruit with the flipper. It turns to poison. You can't mix them together. I heard about an incident where someone did that and he died. I don't know what happened to him, but it mixed together in his stomach, that stinky flipper and canned fruit. A deadly combination.

The walrus won't cross open water to come up on the beach, but if the ice is still thick, they might come up on on the beach if they feel like it. I've seen walrus on the beach. They are gigantic. They weigh a couple of thousand pounds, maybe twenty-five-hundred pounds. They're bigger even than me.

With long tusks, too. Those old ones with the biggest tusks and whiskers look like old men. But we only go after the young ones or the females because the skin is softer. The meat and blubber is softer on females and young ones. Those old guys, man, they are tough. Young bulls are better. The older ones are hard to eat. The meat is sinewy.

Those walrus look like elephants they are so big. When they come near town in summer, they come in large numbers and that is quite a sight to see. I remember seeing what seemed like five hundred of them on one iceberg. This was only a couple of miles out from the center of Barrow. Pretty amazing.

Those five hundred were clustered right together, big hulks all resting together on the ice. And many other walrus were scattered around them. They were everywhere. On that one day I must have seen at least fifteen hundred walrus.

The walrus gives off this very distinct odor, kind of clammy, unbathed odor. Before we can even see them we can smell them and we know there is walrus nearby. Walrus like to eat clams and once we kill them and cut them open you can find clams they just ate. The main staple diet is eating clams. Walrus hides are very rugged. They have thick skins and to cut up the walrus and butcher it we need axes and very sharp knives.

For them to come right up on shore is rare. More regularly they settle in on the ice in the distance. It all depends on the drift of the ice. Whenever people in town say there are walrus out there, they call all their relatives and say get ready to go out and get your share.

Just like hunting seal, you really have to be careful when you point that rifle. It's critical to take aim at the right spot and make sure you have a direct hit. Right below the head. It's better to shoot from behind, the base of the skull, right near the vertebrae. Then they don't move. But you can still get an instant kill from the front. Again, it's important to make sure they don't roll off the ice into the water. You don't want that. If they don't get away altogether, then they're very heavy to pull back on top of the ice.

If the walrus are offshore, we go out in boats. I own a small boat and two or three of us go together. I usually take my brothers with me. I don't go hunting for walrus that often, maybe every couple of years, because I don't eat that much of it.

I think some people believe that we eat seal meat raw or walrus meat raw. Probably saw it in a movie or something. But Inupiat don't eat either one of those types of meat completely raw. Walrus is a tasty food. The top layer of skin, the fat part, is thick, crunchy and chewy when it is cooked.

I go hunting more to get walrus for my parents. They like to eat it, so I'm mostly hunting for them, to provide for them.

One year, I kept going out looking for walrus and I finally found some. We were out in the boat when we came up on them. They were on the other side of the iceberg. And this one walrus was separated from the herd. So I went after him. He was a monster bull, must have weighed twenty-five-hundred pounds. As big as walrus get. I raised my rifle, took aim, and bang. I was standing up in the boat and just as I took the shot the boat hit the ice. I stumbled as I pulled the trigger.

I hit the walrus. The shot seemed perfect, right below the head. And it may have been. But the walrus put its head down, turned its head, and the tusks hit the ice. Then the whole body followed, turning to the side and rolling right into the water.

I saw the way it was happening, that the walrus was going to fall off the ice, and I quickly grabbed for a harpoon. I threw the harpoon and it hit him, but I didn't hit him square and it just bounced off! Or maybe I did hit right and I had just forgotten to sharpen the tip. It came right off, though. Some important lessons to learn there. I lost him. Boy, that was frustrating. That was the big one that got away. The currents quickly took him under.

When people who live far away hear that we hunt in the spring and the summer they probably think we are going out in warm weather. They don't really know Barrow, though. It is hardly ever warm here the way it is other places and often in March when we are hunting it still could easily be twenty degrees below zero. With the whole area very much covered with snow.

When we go hunting we always have to dress as if it is the coldest day of the winter. We dress like that because you know you will be going out there all day and you will be surrounded by ice and when that breeze starts blowing or the sun goes down, it gets really cold, really fast.

I wear thick coveralls, winter boots, gloves, hat and winter parka. There's definitely a hood on that parka. The boots are usually mukluks, the Eskimo-style, handmade boots sewn from furs. And my parka was handmade specially for me by my mother. It's a beautiful blue parka with embroidered decorations and it is very special to me. I try to take good care of it and I don't always wear that parka to go hunting. I try to protect it and keep it clean. It is painstaking to sew a parka. They used to be made only from the skins of animals. But some Canadians studied the way caribou keep warm and created a technique to make hollow fibers that match the way caribou skin and hair combine to keep those animals warm. They tried to figure out how caribou kept warm in the coldest winters and they did. It was right in front of us the whole time.

Caribou sometimes congregate in herds of hundreds of thousands. The way buffalo used to in the old West. Tremendous numbers get together and migrate back and forth across the North Slope of Alaska and into Canada.

One time I found myself in the middle of a herd like that. I was coming home from fish camp in the springtime, May, traveling by snowmachine and carrying a full load of geese. Suddenly, I was in the midst of five thousand or so caribou. Probably more. As far as I could see in every direction, there were caribou. All of a sudden, they were everywhere. I was headed towards Barrow, going north, and the caribou were heading east in the direction of Canada. I popped up over a hill and there they were. I just happened to be right in the middle of their path. It was a shame that I didn't have a camera with me.

I stopped the snowmachine, pulled out a rifle and picked one young male out of the pack. It was the rutting season and I knew I couldn't shoot a bull. I shot one caribou and watched the others go by. I sat there for a long time and they were still coming. Eventually, I started up the snowmachine and drove off. I looked back at them one time and I was still seeing thousands and thousands of caribou.

There were many times before that I saw caribou in bunches of forty or fifty together. There would be that many within view at once, spread over the country. But that time was the only time I ever saw one of the huge herds you hear so much about. As a hunter, I felt I could close my eyes and raise my rifle and just shoot in any direction and be bringing home dinner. I just shot the one, though.

It was quite a sight. Tremendous. Sometimes in nature you see things that don't seem quite real. I just stood in awe of those caribou.

Another kind of animal that comes into the Barrow area sometimes is musk oxen. They only come around once in a blue moon. They are the strangest creatures. They are very wide, with huge heads like buffalo and have very, very thick coats of hair hanging down in what seem to be messy rows. They are built like army tanks. They are low-to-the-ground and kind of look fat. But you know something? They are just about as fast as tanks.

Technically, it's possible to hunt musk ox, but they are fairly rare so you need a government permit and I have never had a permit to get one. The permits are very hard to get. They are very limited. I hardly even know anybody who has hunted them and shot one.

Musk ox travel in herds and they usually don't come much closer to town than twenty-five miles in the region south of Barrow, towards the Brooks Range. They don't look like they could run very fast, but they fool you. Once I was on a snowmachine and I couldn't even keep up with the herd. I couldn't believe it. There were five or six of them together that time and they were flying. I was totally in awe of how fast they could move.

Once in a while moose come around. Near Anchorage, or in the Matanuska-

Susitna Valley in Southcentral Alaska, moose are common and walk right into town, especially during the winter. There are a lot fewer moose up north and it's a special occasion when they show up. I haven't eaten moose very often, though it's a good game meat that is very popular. I would have to get used to it in the same way other Alaskans would have to get used to the fishy taste of the foods popular with the Inupiat. Muktuk, of course, from the whale, is one of our favorite foods and when it's cooked it's kind of like salty beef.

Barrow is much more developed than it used to be when I was young. We relied much more heavily on the food we harvested. We are close to the land because we have always been close to the land. I grew up that way. Things are a little bit different here now. We have restaurants. There is a pizza parlor. There is a Mexican food restaurant. I eat in those restaurants most of the time. And our grocery store is pretty sophisticated. We can get everything we want. Lettuce, salad, donuts, canned goods, deli.

But every year I will go out whaling in the spring and go hunting in the spring and summer. I feel that I need to go. The store-bought food alone will not satisfy my cravings for the food I got used to when I was growing up. If we eat only store-bought food we get fat and lazy.

Subsistence hunting is a lot of work. When we go out in the spring it takes a lot of preparation time. We camp out, supply ourselves with a stove, a tent. That's a lot more challenging than walking down the aisles of the supermarket.

But I like working for my food. It's like the cowboy in Texas who raises beef on a ranch. Cowboys do a lot of work just to herd those animals. If they didn't do it, they wouldn't have supper on the table.

If I was an Eskimo living in Anchorage, I would make sure I came back to Barrow to hunt each year. Or if I couldn't do that, I would make sure I took enough of my foods with me and kept them in the freezer. It wouldn't be good enough for me to shop at a grocery store, or convenience stores for snacks, or go to restaurants for my food. That alone wouldn't be enough.

If I had to, though, I'd eat at Japanese restaurants, eat sushi. That raw fish is pretty much like some of what I eat in Barrow. It's close. One of my grandfathers had some Japanese friends and they would come over his house in Barrow and eat what he was eating. They ate some raw fish, fish that was sitting out in the weather for a little while and was almost mush. It gets real soft and is something our ancestors considered to be a delicacy. And they liked it, too. So that makes me think I could eat sushi to satisfy my hunger for real food.

If I was traveling for a long time and couldn't get the foods I'd like I might get desperate and go into a grocery store. I would buy fish in the frozen food section and just eat it frozen with seal oil.

I have heard some people say their food tastes best when they barbecue it themselves, or eat it after cooking their food on an open fire. For me, food tastes the best when I have hunted for it myself. That way I get to eat the food of my ancestors and eat the food I have eaten my whole life.

Chapter 11

A few years ago, I was out in a boat hunting for ugruk with my younger brother Percy and two cousins when we were almost crushed by the sea ice.

Our elders had told us not to go too far out from shore because they were keeping an eye on the conditions and didn't like what they saw. The wind can shift and the ice can change very rapidly and catch you by surprise. It was a twenty-foot open boat, which is a pretty good sized boat, but compared to the power of the ice, it's nothing.

We had already shot one seal and were going after more when all of a sudden we realized we were nearly surrounded by ice. If the ice closes in, you are trapped. The boat can't move at all and if the ice keeps coming, it can simply crush it, breaking the boat apart into little pieces. And the same thing can happen to you. We were about a mile out from the shore when we saw what was happening. We tried to get the boat to shore real quick, but there was hardly any room to maneuver at all.

Most people don't understand the way sea ice works. They stand on land and look out and see the frozen ocean. It looks flat and still. Which it might be at that moment. But at certain times of the year, when it isn't frozen completely solid, the ice moves a lot. When there is some open water and you are out boating, you have to be very careful. The situation can shift within minutes. If you know your whaling history you have heard stories about how big wooden ships got caught in the ice and just crushed into little bits. That's how we get lumber in town. Those boats back near the start of the twentieth century were ten times or a hundred times bigger than our skinboats. They were like skyscrapers compared to tents. And the whalers weren't safe in them! They had to abandon ship many times.

If you get trapped, sometimes you have to forfeit the boat. That's when the ice moves in completely around you and you can't get back to land in time. When that occurs, your best chance is to get to a really big iceberg and hope and pray that it doesn't break up. You have to leave the boat behind. That's a last resort and you try to avoid doing that.

We were thinking we might have to do it this time, but at the same time I was thinking hard about ways to save us. I was in charge and I tried not to show panic. I kept telling my kid brother and my two cousins to push the boat, to row hard. I tried to keep them busy.

The first thing, I made the decision to dump the seal in the water. It was maybe two hundred pounds of dead weight. I knew that if we threw it overboard we would have a better chance of getting back. We do not like to waste a seal, but the weight was holding us back. It would be easier for us to row. This was a very serious situation and we had no choice. The ice was closing the water near us very fast. It was becoming a life and death matter in a hurry.

We tried to paddle fast, but the ice closed in on us anyway. However, because we got rid of the seal, we were able to jump out of the boat and lift the boat up onto the ice so it didn't get crushed. It was light enough that we could just manage. We stood on the ice and dragged the boat away from that spot and several yards away we were able to put it back into open water. We got back in the boat, paddled it as far as we could until we reached another patch where it was all frozen, and then lifted it out again. We kept doing that over and over, getting closer to land. Our goal was to get ashore, but even before that maybe have someone see us and come out and help.

With the ice closing in fast we had to repeat that lifting and jumping in and out of the boat many times. It was slow going and each time we did it, it was pretty risky.

One time it got really hairy. One of the confusing things to a person if they don't know the area and they aren't used to how the water and ice work is the way the currents flow. The current and the wind can blow the floating sea ice both ways. The ice can crumble right before your very eyes. You might be counting on an iceberg to hold together and it doesn't. One time it got very scary when a big iceberg started moving towards us.

I have seen the ice move very, very fast. When the icebergs get going with a current, it seems just about anything can happen. And you're helpless just sitting there. In the ocean near where I live at the top of the world there are six or seven currents going. We have the Chukchi Sea and the Beaufort Sea meeting together and flowing in opposite directions in some places. It can be very tricky and treacherous to tell what's going on in the water. At the same time, in the middle, the ice might be flowing one way from the Beaufort Sea and the other way from the Chukchi Sea. It can even be like a whirlpool.

The icebergs are huge. They weigh tons and tons and are as large as the biggest buildings in a city like Anchorage. Only, of course, you can't see all of the ice. You have heard the expression "The tip of the iceberg." It's not just an expression, it's really true. Three-quarters of the iceberg is under the water. What most people don't know is that icebergs can turn over at any time. Just flip on the side. So while icebergs can actually rescue you in an emergency if you have to leave your boat, it's really not safe or smart to walk on them. It's those twisting currents which turn them over. You might not be able to stay on one very long.

When we saw this giant iceberg moving our way, just bearing down on us like an oncoming train, we hustled that boat over a patch of ice very quickly. It was pretty intense activity, let me tell you. If we hadn't seen it and acted so fast the iceberg would have crushed us in seconds. It ended up passing about fifty yards behind us. It really was a frightening situation, but I tried not to show how scared I was.

Learning to read the ice is something that comes with the experience of growing up in Barrow. If I were just out there and didn't understand the currents we might have been swimming all day.

Another time during fall whaling, we killed a bowhead whale, one that was about forty feet long, and about twenty boats were towing it to shore. Only we caught it kind of late in the day so it was getting dark and all the boats had spotlights on. We knew we were getting close to Point Barrow and we knew there was ice there and we were aware of one big iceberg moving towards us. We made the judgment that we could outrun it. Only it outran us and ran right into us. The iceberg ran right into our whale.

The berg flowed right into the middle of our boat caravan. The ice missed me by three feet and tore the tow rope and hit the boat next to me. We thought we were moving faster than this iceberg, but it came right up on us and just knocked a few boats out of the way.

You can bet we were scrambling that time. All of a sudden, you look up and there's a giant iceberg right over your head. And I'm there frantically trying to disconnect from the rope and the other boat. I couldn't back up. I had to try to turn to the side. Man, that was scary.

Two boats in the back of the flotilla held fast to the whale until we got some new ropes. We retrieved the whale, tied it back up, and brought it in.

The warnings issued by our elders were true. They told us to watch out for fast icebergs. They told us about icebergs that could outrun our boats, even with outboard motors. They warned us icebergs could run us down and flip us over. It all happened to us that day. One danger is that when a boat is turned over the crew is dumped into the water and the way the currents work they will take a man away right away before he can be saved by the crew of another boat. We found out that even an outboard motor is no match for that kind of current.

We were lucky again that day, though. Nobody was hurt at all. That was kind of a miracle. It was just a close call that startled us.

Chapter 12

There is education and there is education. The education given to you by your parents and your family is one kind. The education that you go to school for is another kind.

Unfortunately, when I was a youngster, the only way to get a real education after grade school was to leave Barrow. Most of the time growing up until then I had been a pretty happy child. But my life got a lot rougher when I had to go somewhere else for school.

All my worst tendencies that had started to show up as a teenager came out even stronger.

When I was growing up, Barrow did not have its own real high school, so a lot of kids went away to learn. During the 1950s and 1960s the Bureau of Indian Affairs funded the school system and the first time it was possible to go to school in grades ten through twelve was 1974. This was true in all of the small communities of the Alaska Bush at that time, and had been that way for years.

Until a law was passed about twenty-five years ago that required the government to build schools in every village so children could be educated in their home towns, the only way to continue your formal education was to move away from your family. Barrow finally got its own high school, a very fancy one costing $70 million, in 1983. They said it was the nicest school in the entire country.

I was scheduled to start high school in 1969, before the change. At that time, many Eskimos were sent to schools outside of Alaska. One place you could go was on an Indian reservation in Oklahoma — my brother Johnny went there — but I didn't want to go to outside of the state. The best school was Mount Edgecumbe in Sitka, the famous school in Southeast Alaska, but there wasn't room for everybody who wanted to go.

When I was in my early teens, I was a pretty wild boy. We had our own gang and we would go around making trouble. It was not much like the kind of gangs you see on television where they go around shooting people. By that measurement we made mischief, not big trouble. But I didn't get good grades in school because I didn't try very hard.

I can't really explain why I had become this kind of teenager. My father and mother had tried to teach me how to behave and I had my grandpa's teachings. But I was listening with my head, not with my heart. So I became a troublemaker.

Kind of late I got excited about going away to school and I thought it would be Mount Edgecumbe. That was the place most people went and the place everyone talked about. They thought it was pretty good there. But I waited too long to apply and there was no room for me there. Then I thought about a school in Oregon, but that didn't work out either. So they sent me to Kodiak.

I didn't know very much about Kodiak then. Kodiak is famous for a few things. It is one of the largest islands in the United States and boy, is the weather different from Barrow. It rains a lot and it's a lot warmer. It gets pretty windy there, too, with the strong wind that blows in from the ocean. It's a center for commercial fishing and one thing everyone has heard about is Kodiak king crab. I think they had more crab there than anywhere else in the whole world. And, everyone knows about the brown bears. Kodiak bears are huge. When they stand on hind legs they can be more than ten feet tall. They are even bigger than polar bears. Sport hunters come from all over the place to Kodiak to go after those bears.

But I didn't know any of those things when I was sixteen. A lot of people think that old system of sending kids away to school was terrible. And it is hard to leave your family behind. But at the same time it sounded pretty exciting to a kid who had never been anywhere. Everybody was talking about me leaving town and I knew I would get to go on an airplane.

I don't know if I was actually really glad to be going, but I was definitely excited about the adventure of it all. In those days, Barrow didn't have a modern airport the way it does now and we caught the plane a few miles outside town at the Naval Arctic Research Laboratory.

But going to Kodiak turned out to be one of the most horrible experiences of my life. I thought there would be other kids like me there, but there weren't. There was only one other Eskimo from another village. And there aren't any

Inupiat Eskimos living in Kodiak.

I was away from home and that didn't help. I didn't really know what to do. I had nobody to talk to. Other kids teased me, tried to take advantage of me and called me names. There was one other kid there who felt sorry for me and talked to me. Her name was Sue. She tried to counsel me and help me because she was from Kodiak and she knew who the bad boys were. She told me they didn't like me, that they were after me and to stay away from them. She was a lot older than me and she had a boyfriend and her boyfriend got jealous.

I only lasted one year there, not even a full year. I got kicked out because I got in a fight with this one kid.

He started calling me names like "Barbaric Eskimo" and we argued. I'd had enough from this kid. That led to a fight. He hit me pretty good and I hit him back. I was bigger. He was a short, stocky kid, but he was muscular. They thought I was going to hurt him pretty bad. I stopped fighting, but I got the worst of it. They didn't like me there. I was Native and he was white and so I got punished and he didn't get anything. I defended myself and he didn't get punished. But he was white. That says it all. It didn't seem fair that I was the only one being punished. The principal whipped me with a "board of education." A big, intimidating board. He hit me until I started to bleed on my behind. Then they sent me home. They should either have given us both lashes, or sent us both home. I didn't want to get sent home. I wanted to go after that principal, but I went home instead.

I stayed home for a few months and then they sent me to high school in Fairbanks. I enrolled at Lathrop. Fairbanks may be the second largest city in Alaska, but it's a lot more like Barrow than Kodiak is. It's very cold in the winter, just like Barrow, and a lot of Natives live there. That made a lot more sense.

Lathrop was not nearly as bad as being at Kodiak, but I was a troubled kid in those days so I had my problems. I knew a lot of people in Fairbanks, so that was good, but we were still living in foster homes, away from our real parents. It felt crowded for me there. Man, it was too crowded.

Things got pretty tense at school, as well. We divided up along racial lines, whites, blacks and Natives, and had our own groups. I made friends with one guy who was into karate. He made friends with me because of my size. Intimidation, you know. I was running with him. At that time I was already more than six feet tall and weighed at least a hundred-and-eighty pounds. I was strong. The black guys and the Native guys would gang fight after school. I had a lot of anger in me then, a lot of rage.

When you are that age life seems pretty complicated. I had grown up with Eskimos and in an Eskimo culture. This was all new to me. There was a lot of discrimination in Fairbanks then. Prejudice was a big problem. Even at school we were not allowed to be part of the sports teams, it seemed. We tried to get in, but the coaches didn't want us, I felt.

I did make friends with this one black guy who was a really good ballplayer and he'd always tell me I should play football. We'd play pickup games of football and I would just deck everybody. I figured with my size that was one sport I would be good at, but I never got the opportunity to play for the school.

Until I left Barrow I had no idea about this type of discrimination. It totally blindsided me. I had to learn fast or be eaten. I had to learn how to stay out of serious trouble and about certain people who would hurt me. One time in Fairbanks a gang of white kids who were drunk stopped in front of me and began hassling me. They brought out baseball bats. It was an ethnic thing, but they mistook me for somebody else who they wanted to beat up. They started to come after me because I was just in the wrong place and I had to think fast. And talk fast.

I told them I was just walking down the road and had come from my aunt's house. I was just minding my own business. I told them, "I didn't do anything to you guys. I have never seen you before. I don't know you. You're confusing me with someone else. I'm just going home."

They almost started swinging their bats at me, but at the last minute one of the guys said, "He's not the one we want. C'mon, let's go." And they let me go. So much hatred. I was angry, but I was scared.

I was so miserable. I had seen bad things happen when people I knew back home drank too much alcohol, but that didn't stop me. I was a headstrong kid and I was going to do whatever I wanted to. Drinking was an escape. Isn't it for most people who drink too much? There were lots of people who told me not to drink and I knew what was right and wrong, but that didn't stop me. I drank a lot in those days.

One important thing came out of this period of time at Lathrop. Because of all the racial divisions, it made me more proud to be Native. Since everyone seemed to have their own culture, we started a Native culture club. I got heavily involved in that.

In 1972, after I had been at Lathrop a couple of years, it looked like I might be able to become an exchange student and go to Japan. That would have been a thrilling experience. But I screwed it up. I got caught drinking and was sent home to Barrow as punishment. I went home for a month or two and never went back to high school. I just dropped out. It took me until 1980 before I finally got my general equivalency degree.

After a couple of months hanging around in Barrow, I went to a job training program in Kicking Horse, Montana. That's where I got my training to drive heavy equipment.

You might say I got a college degree in life and a graduate degree, too, without ever getting an actual high school diploma.

Chapter 13

I may not have been a great student all of my high school years, but I sure did learn a lot about drinking.

I drank most of the time when I was in high school in Fairbanks. A lot of beer and a lot of whiskey. Very quickly I found out that getting drunk means losing control of yourself and that when someone loses control of himself, it can lead to trouble.

High school turned into a shocking experience for me. What had seemed like it was going to be a great adventure when I set out from Barrow turned into an awful disappointment. I discovered prejudice and discrimination were everywhere and I started drinking quite a bit to cope with my problems.

Back in Barrow, people got drunk and wise people counseled against drinking. I heard the words, but I was going my own way then. People told me not to get messed up with alcohol, but I had never experienced it. Until I experienced drinking too much I didn't believe it could cause so much trouble. I really didn't believe them, I guess. I had an attitude, "I'll find out for myself."

It was mostly beer for me at first, then whiskey. Eventually, I drank a lot of bourbon, but that was later. During high school, drinking was pretty much done on weekends. I could have got into a lot more trouble than I did. A couple of times I landed in jail in Fairbanks for disorderly conduct, for just being drunk on the street downtown. But when I got drunk I got enraged and broke things. I was dangerous to be around. I could have been jailed for that. I was one of the luckier ones. I could have done myself harm, as some people did, or hurt other people. It would have been easy for something to happen and be sent to prison for a long time.

One time I was originally charged with assault. I was so drunk I was essentially blacked out. I didn't know what I was doing. I was fortunate that the charges were eventually dropped.

I had a friend in school who did his best to make me see that I was messing up my life. He took hold of me with both hands and spoke some sense to me, but I didn't listen as well as I should have.

When I think back to those times, it seems as if it was a different Big Bob Aiken living my life. That was a different man, a different human being. For a couple of reasons. I didn't know myself that well at the time. I wasn't comfortable with who I was. The situation I was in without my friends and family left me lonely. And also, there was so much prejudice against Eskimos I got discouraged. Don't forget peer pressure. Drinking was the thing to do.

I drank as much as I did, I guess, because I was disappointed in life and confused. I was sixteen and seventeen years old and I had a lot of frustration. The peer pressure got to me. And I think it's even worse today for kids. The main thing now is sex for teenagers. Alcohol, too, but peer pressure is stronger for sex. They say if you're not doing it, you're not anybody.

If I could do high school all over again I know I would do it totally differently.

The best part of high school was starting the Native culture club. In a sense, that was the start of me being truly connected to my heritage. And that later led me away from alcohol.

I learned a lot about Inupiat culture growing up, of course, but that was in the normal course of events, following the teachings of my parents. But in Fairbanks, it was different. I had to struggle for my identity and I found it comforting to fall back on my heritage, which was being challenged. Starting up the culture club and being an active member brought me to a new horizon and opened my eyes a bit about being proud of who I was. I got a clear picture of that pride in the culture club.

We did a lot of stuff. We collected artifacts. We did Native games. We'd make things ourselves and we'd hold youth rallies. For the first time in so many years school began to get exciting. Being in school started to mean more to me than it had. Much more. I was into learning about myself, about my people. Even if it wasn't part of the regular curriculum, it was coming to me through school. It was probably 1971, after I'd been mostly away from home for two years.

That was the best part of high school in Lathrop. Even though I had a bad time in Kodiak, there was one good thing there. I played a lot of basketball and I was pretty good. I got to show off my skills, though I never did get a chance to play on the school basketball team in Fairbanks.

But I found answers for myself in Native culture and sport instead of basketball. These things made me feel better about myself.

I said that I would like to take high school over again, get a second chance at it, and a lot of that stems from the time I wasted drinking. But I also didn't focus on my classroom learning, either, so that was wasted time. I had the opportunity and the brains to do much more than I did.

Part of the problem was the misunderstandings between Natives and whites. We were Natives fitting into a white school plan. There were so many things I could not understand after coming from Barrow. And there were too many things we were made to do that I wasn't prepared for. Like speech class. Being shy and from a village community, I wanted no part of that. No way. I didn't want to speak in front of the whole class.

When it was my turn, I would just blurt out a little speech, say a few words, and try to get out of there as fast as I could. The teachers were somewhat sympathetic, though, I think. They kind of let me get away with doing it that way. But I still didn't like being up there in front of everyone talking. It was kind of hard.

At the time I thought they were doing me a favor letting me do it the easy way, but I suppose it would have been more beneficial for me in the long run if they'd forced me to make more speeches. I could have done away with my shyness. As everyone who knows me now is aware of, if you let me near a microphone I can be a dangerous dude. I'm not so shy anymore. No. That's wrong. I'm still shy. I just got more brave. I had to do it and I made myself.

I began talking more because I didn't want anybody to misunderstand me. To make sure of that I had to speak up. I feel I was misunderstood in high school, especially by the other students. They thought I was dumb. I was drinking and getting in trouble and I didn't know how to speak up. I didn't know any better.

There was a counselor at Lathrop who helped me a lot. When we met he told me that I could learn a lot more than I was. He told me I was smarter than I was acting. They always said I scored well on those national tests and that if I just put my head together and focused I could do much better. The counselor said I wasn't even trying. Focus on education and you will go far, he said.

I agreed with him. I heard him, but I didn't take any steps to do anything about it. I was too far gone, I thought.

In some ways the old system of uprooting kids and taking them away from their families was bad, but in some ways it was good. The kids who went away to school and really worked to get an education, to take advantage of the opportunities at Mount Edgecumbe, did well.

My cousins all went to boarding school outside of Barrow and they seem to be well-educated. But looking at the kids around Barrow today, they seem to be dropping out of school like flies. They're still in town and live with their parents, and maybe not facing the kind of discrimination I did, but they are still drinking and skipping school.

It would be easy to say that building schools in every community was a better idea, but I'm not sure. I don't know if what is going on today is working any better. I am not too impressed with what I see of today's youth in school. I still see kids who volunteer to go to Mount Edgecumbe. It puzzles me that they want to leave their homes, but they do.

Perhaps the times have changed. In the old days, the students who left to go to school were forced to go. They didn't have a choice. And they were leaving behind a way of life, the subsistence lifestyle so important to our people. Now that lifestyle is fading a bit and maybe young people think they are better off if they get a chance at a good education somewhere else.

When I went to school in Fairbanks, I could have been more successful if I had had a different attitude. It was up to me. Totally up to me. I see that now, but I didn't then. The discrimination surprised me, though. That was the fire that put out my goals.

Leaving Barrow for my high school adventure, one of the most exciting things on my mind was that I would get to see trees. Seems like a simple thing, but I wanted to see trees. I had never seen them. I saw plenty of trees in Kodiak, but once I got out of Barrow I was quickly discouraged.

As a child, my dad took myself and my older brother out on the tractor he drove on his job hauling trash to the dump. I sat on one side and my brother sat on the other side of the CAT. We would be going along and take turns steering when he said we could. I was really impressed by that. And that told me I wanted to be a heavy equipment operator, even if I went to school somewhere else.

It was great just to be with my dad and seeing what he did for a living. Cool stuff. I could control the big machinery.

I didn't really have any other goals when I went to Kodiak, but when I was going to school in Fairbanks I thought about being a welder. I took some vocational ed classes in that. I always knew that I would come back to Barrow, though, once I learned my craft.

In 1975, I spent about nine months in Montana learning the basics of how to drive heavy equipment, road graders and things like that. There was no training facility like it in Alaska yet.

During that period of my life when I was doing everything wrong, that was the smartest thing I did. It's a good thing I went there. I don't know where my wisdom came from to do that. It must have dropped from the sky.

Montana was interesting, but it was not the first time I had been outside of Alaska. By then I had already made a trip to Washington, D.C. through Native Youth Olympics. NYO is the same kind of Native games competition as World Eskimo-Indian Olympics held once a year in Anchorage. Only it is held for teenagers, high school competitors. The culture club steered me to NYO and I did well there since I had a background in the games from Barrow.

When I was eighteen there was a huge festival in Washington gathering people from all over the world, a multi-cultural celebration, and I was picked as one of the Alaska athletes to go and demonstrate Native sports. I did the finger pull, the stick pull, and a lot of other games.

I had not spent a lot of time thinking about going to other places, except for Japan. I came close to having that chance through Lathrop until I got into trouble for drinking. They were not going to send anybody anywhere who was drinking, never mind to a foreign country.

Of course I knew Washington, D.C. was the capital of the country and I did a lot of reading about it. I wanted to see the Washington Monument. I was kind of excited to see the sights. We were also told we would meet all kinds of people from all over the world. I said, "Let's go!"

We were there for a week or more and I did get to see the Washington Monument. And the White House, too. They told us we couldn't take pictures, but I did, anyway. Sneaky, huh?

This trip made a big impact on me. I did get to meet people from other cultures and thought that was fascinating and a lot of people got to meet me and they acted like that was fascinating. There were a lot of curious people there.

There was one older Native man with us who made baskets and a lot of people wanted to know about him, but he didn't speak any English. Not one word. He could understand their English, but couldn't say anything back to them. So I interpreted for him. I helped him out and we started to pal around, but after a while we started to get tired of all the questions.

One of the lady tourists asked me if we still lived in igloos and I couldn't help myself. I said, "Oh yeah." I started getting wise with her. "Sure," I said, "I've got a two-story one. Made it with nice, fresh ice. They make good picture windows." And she said, "Really?" And we laughed, me and the old man, then apologized and told the truth.

It was fun. I thought about letting her walk away believing it. I suppose I was mean back then, a smart aleck kid.

That festival was quite an experience. I found out that there are a lot of people who appreciated our culture, even those who lived thousands of miles away. It was interesting to be appreciated so far from Alaska where I'd seen discrimination.

The people in the Lower 48, and even Alaska, were curious out of ignorance. A person who wants to learn can become a friend. They like to find out things they know nothing about. It would have been interesting to see how I would have been treated in Japan if I had had the chance to go. It would have been a completely different culture for me.

When I finished learning how to drive heavy equipment in Montana, I took a month of truck driving. I joined the Teamsters Union and I got certificates for each one. I was certified in both.

I went directly to work in Barrow and I saw the worst discrimination of my life against Eskimos right where I live. Companies that were owned by our own Native corporation wouldn't give shareholders who live in Barrow the same job opportunities. They'd bring in all the workers from Texas and Seattle instead. They'd bring in workers who had never driven a dump truck and we'd have to teach them. There was a long line of Eskimos who wanted work and they wouldn't get it. I really wondered what was up. It was frustrating.

The Native Corporations were formed out of the Alaska Native Claims Settlement Act in 1971 and what happened was they were contracting out a lot of building work. These were Native corporations running the jobs and the contractors were hiring whites and squeezing out Eskimos. I finally went to my boss and complained and then some of us went to the main offices of the Native Corporation.

We asked what the heck kind of company they were running. There was a lot of questioning and we embarrassed them. I was a shareholder. They finally got rid of some of those guys and turned over some of the work to us. You learn something all the time.

All Photos are by Lew Freedman

Big Bob and several of his nephews at the tip of the United States where the Chukchi Sea and the Beaufort Sea come together.

Big Bob in the hand-made parka his mother made for him.

Muktuk and Mukluks 81

Big Bob standing under the famous whalebones on Barrow's shore by the Arctic Ocean.

82 *Muktuk and Mukluks*

Big Bob drives heavy equipment and that equipment is bigger than even him.

Big Bob Aiken, The World's Largest Eskimo.

Robert and Martha Aiken, Big Bob's parents.

DANGER: POLAR BEARS!
NO VEHICLES BEYOND THIS POINT!
DISTURBING THE BEARS NEAR THE POINT MAY CAUSE THEM TO RETURN TO BARROW AND THE DUMP AREA
PLEASE HELP REDUCE THE CHANCE OF HUMAN INJURY

You've got to keep your eyes peeled in Barrow.

Muktuk and Mukluks 83

The place to stay in town.

The North Slope Borough government logo symbolizes most of the important things in Barrow.

The memorial to Will Rogers and Wiley Post, who died in a plane crash in Barrow in 1935, is a popular tourist attraction.

Barrow is pretty far from everywhere.

84 *Muktuk and Mukluks*

Big Bob draws a crowd during one of the audience participation dances at the World Eskimo-Indian Olympics.

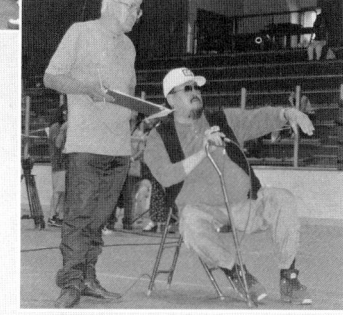

Big Bob (seated) with WEIO offcial George Bennett.

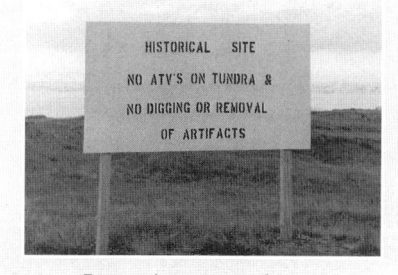

Barrow's got some history to check out.

The remains of a whale carcass on the beach near some jumbled ice.

Big Bob with friend and star WEIO athlete Nicole Johnston.

Now that he's retired from competition, Big Bob frequently works as a judge at WEIO competitions.

Big Bob and Greg Nothstine at WEIO in Fairbanks.

Big Bob and Greg Nothstine demonstrate the stick pull, one of Bob's best events.

86 *Muktuk and Mukluks*

A microphone in hand brings out the sense of humor in Big Bob.

A landmark local church in Barrow.

Big Bob admires the medal won by champion two-foot high kicker Brian Randazzo at WEIO.

Just a small percentage of the medlals Big Bob won as an active athlete.

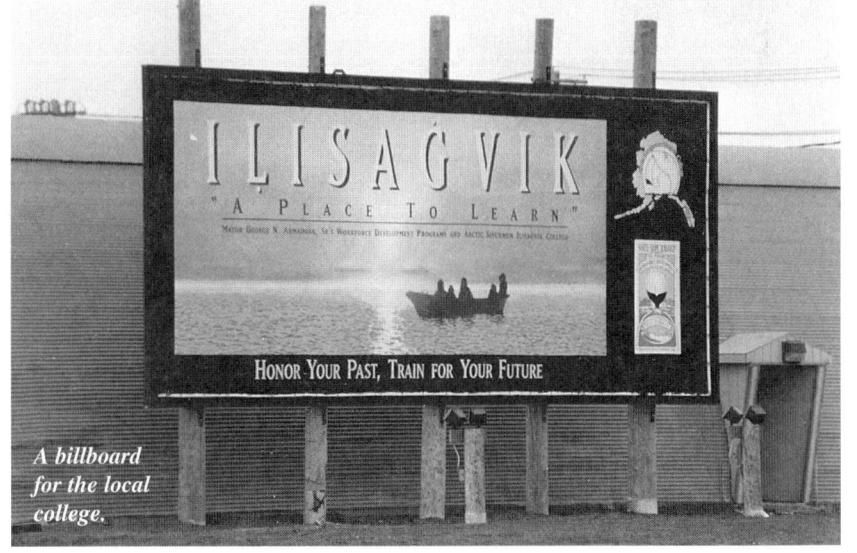

A billboard for the local college.

Muktuk and Mukluks 87

Fran Tate's renowned Barrow Mexican restaurant.

The end-of-season whaling festival attracts everyone in Barrow.

One of the main structures in the Browerville section of Barrow, dating back to whaling ship days in the late 19th century.

Chapter 14

Alcohol has been a big part of things in Barrow my whole life. When I was a kid I remember a lot of people who would die frozen. They would get so drunk they passed out in the street and before anyone could find them, or even knew they were missing, they would freeze to death.

It happened a lot. Once, I found an individual lying on the ground and carried him home half-frozen. Alcohol has been a big issue in my town and a big curse that influenced lots of things. The issue of whether or not Barrow should be a dry town where alcohol is forbidden splits the town.

Barrow has been dry and it has been damp in recent years. We have had several votes and it went back and forth. The elders spoke up against it and that helped. Once, for a little while, several years ago, Barrow was wet. After I came back to town following high school I was actually a clerk in a liquor store. And I was a bouncer in the first bar in town.

There are no liquor stores or bars in Barrow now. They are prohibited. You can't buy or sell alcohol in town. The law says you get arrested for it. But, of course, people know it is still possible to get a drink if they really want it. Liquor gets smuggled in on the jet plane. It happens. Only the most naive person would think that it doesn't ever happen.

There is evidence all around. You can tell when you see someone who has had a lot to drink and he walks funny. Or he sounds funny. Or worse, if he passes out and falls down. That is how drinking too much alcohol can kill you.

Alcohol has always been around us, as long as I can remember. I was thirteen years old when I saved that man's life, picked him up and took him home. That man was one of my relatives. Alcohol has always been a heartache for us.

One time a few years ago I found a frozen stiff. A friend of mine was renting a place and we went over to the house. All the lights were out, but the door was open. We found a light bulb and turned it on and there was a guy lying there frozen solid. Dead on the floor of the house.

It was a man we knew, a local drunk. When I checked him out he was frozen stiff. It was just like hitting your knuckles against a wooden table. Dead as a doornail. So many depressing things like that have happened in Barrow because of liquor.

When you are a youngster you don't always recognize all the horrible things going on around you. I know I didn't think much about alcohol in Barrow when I was a boy. It was just another thing that was around us, like snow and ice. You grow up with that, accepting that as part of everyday reality that everybody drank.

I began drinking when I was in high school in Fairbanks. I drank a lot of whiskey. You might think I had seen a lot of bad things because of alcohol and that would teach me not to drink, but it wasn't like that. I drank anyway. Everyone drank. When things were going badly at that age and all my friends were drinking it seemed easier to drink than not to drink. Sure, there were many examples of bad things happening that I had seen, and many people had told me how bad drinking was, but I just had to try it myself.

I remember trying alcohol for the first time and I got a buzz and I sort of liked the buzz. It's also hard not to drink when drinking involves a lot of your friends. Peer pressure is hard to resist. You actually think you are having fun and you are being social and cool. Alcohol was a natural part of the relationship with friends.

As an adult, from a distance, I can see how that was the wrong thing to do and, of course, now I am telling young people to ignore this very same kind of peer pressure from their friends.

At least I speak from experience. I am also asking parents to exert influence over their children so they won't drink. Not too many people from my family talked to me that way at first and urged me not to drink. Sadly, no, that didn't happen. Perhaps they never had a clue that they should.

Drinking was a big mistake in my life, one of the biggest mistakes I ever made. But if I had never experienced it, I wouldn't be able to know how to help others trying to quit. I know because I had to do that myself.

If you lived your whole life in the Alaska Bush the way I have, you will know people whose lives were ruined by alcohol. You will know people who have died because of alcohol. People close to you. It has happened to me. I lost some cousins because of alcohol not too many years ago.

One of my cousins who had just finished high school was drinking a lot and got into heavy metal music. One day he was drunk and he started arguing with his nephews. He went into his bedroom and shot himself with a gun. He was very drunk. And just think, we had to clean up his remains from the room so his parents wouldn't have to see that. That's hard.

I think the music contributed, too, all those negative lyrics. I saw all those heavy metal negative lyrics pour into his mind. He wasn't very popular with girls and he was just a loner. Then he got drunk and this one argument set him off and he shot himself. Sad.

You have to be very strong to give up drinking once you have started. Drinking leads to more drinking and that just leads to more drinking. It becomes easier and easier to keep drinking. I am a big man and I could drink a lot, just the way I can eat a lot.

Drinking was very bad for me. I drank so much I couldn't always remember what I did. Drinking clearly wasn't doing me any good at all. I kept hearing that I was hurting other people. Each time I sobered up, other people approached me and said, "Do you remember you did this to me?" Or "Do you remember you said that to me?" I couldn't recall any of what they were saying. I didn't know.

I had blackouts. I couldn't remember my own actions. I might have hit someone, or beat someone up, and I wouldn't remember. When that happens that's pretty scary. I drank for a long time. For many years. There was a lot of pain involved. It took a long time to learn my lesson and a long time to conquer my willingness to drink. That little buzz I got the first time definitely wasn't worth it. By the time I stopped drinking completely I was thirty-five years old.

I did it with my own willpower. One day I just realized that I was ruining my life by drinking, that drinking had taken over the real me. I had had enough suffering and I knew I had to stop. So I just quit. Just like that. I was taking responsibility for myself. I just didn't think there was any reason to drink.

You might think there was a tremendous struggle to stop drinking after all that time, but it wasn't that hard. I could resist alcohol once I put my mind to it. I started going to church and that helped me at the time.

Alcohol has been a terrible thing for the Eskimos of Barrow. I have seen alcohol do so much damage to people I know, or love, or am close to, friends, just people I grew up with, it has hurt them all over a long period of time.

I picture it this way: if everybody in Barrow lived in one house, that house would have burned to the ground. To nothing. That's how bad I feel about things.

Just knowing that you have lost the whole house. Sometimes it feels as if a house you have built over years, from day one, burned all the way to the ground in just a few hours. That's the kind of feeling it leaves me with.

You used to be able to buy alcohol in Barrow in package stores and bars, and they are long gone, but you can still buy liquor because bootleggers bring it in. They charge a hundred-and-fifty dollars for a fifth of vodka. There is a law against it, but it still comes in. Everyone thinks they can stop it, but no one has.

The liquor comes in with groceries a lot of times. I think the liquor stores outside of the city must be sneaking it in with the groceries. Bootleggers are professionals. They make sure that if you want alcohol in Barrow you can get it.

In the mid-1990s, Barrow took two votes that affected the law on possession of alcohol in town. The first vote, which was very close, was to let people have liquor. The second vote, a year later, was to ban liquor, to be totally dry. We are totally dry. I am thankful for the second vote. I am relieved.

When the first vote occurred, I was horrified. I just saw so much more heartache coming our way. A preacher preached that you can't stop the world from going around, that you can't stop the alcohol from coming to town. He was saying that if people are desperate enough there are ways they can get their alcohol. It comes down to all we can do is pray. That's all we can do.

There are many ways of thinking about this. When it looked like liquor might be legal and that bars might open in Barrow again, I got the idea that maybe I would just buy up three or four liquor licenses and hang them on the wall of my bedroom. Help shut it down that way. But I know there is always going to be alcohol in town no matter what you do and you can pray a lot and witness a lot, but there will still be liquor.

I do not go around town telling adults they should not drink anymore. It wouldn't be right. I think it is important to influence young people not to start, but you can't control older people. They make their own decisions about their own lives. You can't order them around. But the one thing you can show them is how to lead a sober life. That's what I do. I think of that as being a witness, as someone proving he can live a sober life in the midst of all this alcohol.

The way I feel about it is you can move to Anchorage if you want alcohol because there's alcohol all over the place there. Everywhere you turn in Anchorage, there's alcohol readily available. And you can stay away from it there, too. Maybe because Anchorage is a bigger place. There may be liquor stores and bars everywhere in the city, but you don't have to go in.

Somebody said that they had a dream that there were all these liquor stores and bars in Barrow open for business, but that all of the people were just staying away from them. They were right there, but people ignored them. Nobody was buying alcohol even though they could. I thought about that, but if that were ever to be true it would be a miracle. I guess that is a dream of faith.

To me alcohol stopped being equated with getting a buzz on a long time ago. To me now alcohol is equated with sadness. I see it this way: I picked up a pretty flower and I wanted it to blossom into a rose. So I put it into the water, only it was alcohol. Pure grain alcohol. And a few minutes later the flower crumpled up and died. Just fell over.

I think that's what happens to us when beautiful girls consume alcohol. Some of my young classmates who were so cute, in a matter of years they shriveled up and look older than I do. From alcohol. Just alcohol. They are not so pretty now. They don't take care of themselves or their kids. They're just dying. Dying of the cancer of alcohol. Their kids are alcoholics now. Their kids are having babies and their babies are born with fetal alcohol syndrome. They're alcoholics before they're even born.

Seeing all of this happening solidifies my resolve to live my life sober, to impart the wisdom of our elders, and to carry on our culture. I am trying to show that sobriety is an alternative lifestyle to alcohol. And what I want to show young people is that you can't do the Native games at the World Eskimo-Indian Olympics and succeed if you drink. You cannot do anything that is a strength event or a high kick if you are getting high.

I have been sober for a decade. If I were to show up at someone's house right now and ask for a drink my friends would think I lost my mind. I think they would faint. One gal wouldn't, though. She would be overjoyed. She would gladly serve me a drink. You see at the same time I try to show people they can do without alcohol, some of them try to tell me that I'd be the life of the party if I did drink.

My friends wouldn't believe it at first if I asked for a drink, or at second, either. I have been sober so long. But setting an example is hard. There are a lot of things you give up. A lot of things that you are used to, like when you start seeing people come around you used to know. You can't be friends with them now because they drink and you don't.

One thing that always makes me feel good, though, is when little kids come right up to me and say — "Hi, Big Bob!" — and wave at me. It's a good feeling to know that you are being an example for others. And you hope to God that they will follow you. That's all you can do. Hope they follow your example and not the example of others who have made their lives focus on alcohol.

I feel that the people who were my classmates are on their own. They are grown up. But I think if we reach our children, and we train them right, I don't think they will take the path that leads to that unhealthy lifestyle. If they have somebody to go to, if they have something to fall back on, a good example, they can see a way out.

Chapter 15

Learning about the Native games in Barrow from my father and uncles really helped me when I was in high school in the 1970s and we formed a team from Barrow to compete at the statewide Native Youth Olympics in Anchorage.

Right away, I dominated. I won four gold medals, in the arm pull, stick pull, Indian stick pull and in leg wrestling. It should be no surprise that they were all events that involved a lot of strength. Those always were my best kind of events.

I had paid my dues in the games as a youth before I got away from my home town and that made a big difference when I started to compete in Fairbanks and Anchorage. I had a head start.

The chance to compete in sports that represented our people was a big deal to me since I wasn't involved in other team sports in Fairbanks. Plus, I already had experience.

Just going to a gathering like that was exciting for me. This was at a time when I was facing a lot of discrimination and here was an opportunity to be with others like me and to shine some light on our colorful culture.

I remember there was an all-Indian band there from Arizona which traveled all over the world. "Xit" was their name. They were a really good band. Here it was my first time at NYO and they stopped the music in the middle and called me up to the stage and introduced me as the guy who won four gold medals. All these people started clapping and cheering. I was so proud. Then the guy from the band wanted to leg wrestle me, just kidding around.

The Native Youth Olympics was a big event and I was impressed with what was going on. I knew coming to Anchorage that we would be competing against a lot of people. And we were dominating the games! We went around challenging everybody that we would win these games for the north. But even then we made a point of telling everybody that these were games that were given to us by our elders.

Winning was also very good for my self-esteem. Before going to NYO I thought we were just going to be competing against athletes from Anchorage and I thought, "Man, no problem." I didn't know that we would be competing against the whole state, and I didn't really understand the significance of that. The Eskimos of the north figured to do well because these were our games, but when we beat everybody, I thought, "Wow!" It wasn't until we were marching in that I truly realized all the athletes who were competing. Some of those guys looked tough, too. But we beat most of them.

I love the Native Youth Olympics and I think they are a very good event for young people not only in Anchorage and Fairbanks, but from all over the Bush. It's a good introduction to the games and our heritage. In recent years, teaching of the culture of the games has become part of the elementary school curriculums in many places in Alaska. That's a good thing, too. All kids who live in Alaska should learn about their ancestors.

After I grew up and stopped competing in NYO and retired from the World Eskimo-Indian Olympics, I became a Native Youth Olympics official and coach. I enjoy doing that, but one thing worries me about NYO. Over the years, some officials have tried to change the games and make them easier. That's wrong. We should never do that. They have a purpose and we should not tamper with the purpose. It's uncalled for. You can't simplify the games. That would be like taking our survival skills away.

I asked the other officials if they would humbly approach the elders to ask them very politely if they could change things. That would be one thing. If you explain to the elders what you're trying to do and why you want to make changes and if they agree with you, then it's okay. But otherwise it is not right.

People consider me a purist. I don't think change is open to question. The way to do the games has been given to us. In other regions, like Canada, they may do things a little bit differently, but when you live in Alaska and the games come from here, they have a direct link to the lifestyle we live. I see the elders going, "No, no, no. Do it right."

I think some of them would turn over in their graves if they were to see how some games have been changed already. We must remember these games have a direct connection to our survival. I don't think you should mess with that at all. We are unqualified, unworthy to change the games. That means we would have to change our lifestyle. Or when it came time to rely on what we learned from the games helping us in subsistence, we would not be able to do it.

I think it lessens us to simplify the games. The games reflect the way we adapt to our environment. We should not adapt the games to the modern environment. If the games are simplified and made easier for people, then there is no sense in having them.

The four-man carry is one game I saw simplified. I disagreed with some officials who wanted to let the competitors use straps. In this game the competitor must carry four people who weigh about one-hundred-and-fifty pounds each. One thing that makes it hard is each person has to balance and sometimes they slip. Well, I've seen where they allow the men to be strapped on to the carrier so they wouldn't slip. I saw where they used chairs to let them climb up. Then everybody would jump on. That's just not done. It's too easy. That's not the right way. Traditionally, how it is done is you lift the four people off the ground at once. That's like lifting four seals around you and carrying them away over the ice ridges. And those seals would be dead meat. Those seals aren't going to jump off chairs. They're dead.

This should not be happening, but one reason it does happen is the kind of times we live in. The world seems to be looking for an easier approach to do things. People aren't willing to work as hard as they used to. In this case, I notice the up-and-coming athletes say the way we are doing things is too hard. We've got to improve it, they say. Improve it. Those are the words that were used.

I would say the changes are making things easier, not improved. Always I have to keep reminding people the games are supposed to be hard. When people come to me and talk about "improving" things I sit them down and make them listen to the story behind a particular game. I give them the rundown. This is important. This is how we play the games. I remember when I was a young buck I was the same way. I said something about changing a game and an elder came right up to me and shook a finger in my face.

It's all about modern conveniences. Everybody wants to do things the easier way. Sometimes that's good. It makes sense to have snowmachines instead of dog teams. But just because something is newer doesn't mean it's better. Other regions of the state have changed the games and when they come to Native Youth Olympics they have to be corrected. I had a big dispute a couple of years ago with an official about the scissors broad jump. In the scissors broad jump you take off with both feet, land on one foot with the other behind it, and then you come back around, land on the second foot and jump forward. This is what you do if you are out hunting on the frozen ocean and you have to jump between ice floes. The way they were doing it was just like the hop, skip and jump in track and field. I told this guy, "This is not the triple jump and we are not doing 'Wide World of Sports.' This is the Arctic sports scissors broad jump. Do it right."

I was there as the Barrow coach, but I told them I didn't want any part of it. I said, "I am not going to allow you to change the games. But if you are going to allow this to happen, I will just back away and just go sit down by my team."

You get a lot more distance with the triple jump. Maybe that's why they liked it. But there's a huge difference. I tried to explain that, but they didn't catch on. I feel I have a responsibility to be a guardian of the tradition, especially if I am a coach or an official, a responsibility to my elders.

The games are a matter of life and death in the real world. That's how serious they are. Think of it this way: if you are doing the triple jump instead of the scissors broad jump when you are hunting, you could land in the ocean and be in real trouble. I don't think the people from "Wide World of Sports" would be able to survive up here in the north. There's a reason why there is a difference between their survival skills and ours. They live in warm weather and we live in the coldest weather known to man.

There are several things involved. Respect for the elders and tradition. The learning of survival skills. And the preservation of the past. It is hard because it is supposed to be hard. It always was hard to survive in the north. I feel it's my duty to inform people of that and what I learned.

Remember how it was. In the past they had to know their offspring would be able to survive in the winter and survive after their parents were gone. If they were out on their own, what would their instincts be? The games are the test of their ability and agility and their mind and body control when they are alone in the wilderness with nowhere to go. If you panicked, you would not survive very long. If you didn't have a survival instinct, you ceased to exist. The games are about the survival instincts we need to have. The games help create them in us.

You inherit survival skills from your family, from living hard and playing hard. And you are taught survival skills as an insurance by the elders who know what it's like out there and what it takes to survive up north.

We do have modern conveniences in many ways. Our boats have motors, our rifles are more sophisticated, our snowmachines go fast. But what happens if the motor breaks on the boat, or the snowmachine breaks down?

These games bring out the best in you. What can you endure? There's a lot of pain, but man has got to know his limitations in case he is put in a situation where he must cope with great danger. It is important to know the extent of your own abilities if you are stranded. That's why the games are not to be trifled with. I have always believed this, but I also know it from personal experience.

In 1985, I was out duck hunting on the ice with a snowmachine when I got hurt.

I was very heavy then, very obese, and I had a hernia that ruptured. It ripped inside me. It felt like my intestines were coming out. I was ten miles out of town when it happened and I was in terrible pain.

I shot a duck and when I reached out for it, I just split my stomach wall open. I stood there for a while in intense pain. I realized after a little while that it was up to me to get myself home. If I had not tested myself before, I might have just laid down right there and waited for somebody to come by. But there was nobody around and there was no reason to think anyone would come. It was just as likely that a polar bear would start nosing around and see me there.

I didn't want to lie down. I knew if I did I wouldn't be able to get up again. My body really wanted to just rest, but I wouldn't give in. I held one hand under my stomach to try to hold my intestines in tightly and I just left the duck right there.

It was hard to start my snowmachine. I had one hand on the throttle and tried to steer and do everything one-handed. I barely started it. My vision was getting blurry and it was getting worse and worse. I felt faint. I thought I was bleeding inside badly and I could feel myself going downhill fast. I got the snowmachine moving, but every bump on the road was sheer agony. I wanted to scream. I wanted to stop, but I knew I had to get home. Finally, I rode right up to my door and crawled into the house. I crawled up to the couch and called 911 for an ambulance.

It would be nice to say that I thought about the games during the ordeal, but I didn't think about them at all. That's not the point. It was natural instinct that was developed inside of me because of the games, to get back to civilization and get help. But being strong was an important part of that. Mentally as well as physically. You know you want to survive, but you have to tell your body to move.

You are at your strongest when you are young, but you get stronger mentally as you get older and have experience. It would be ideal if those things developed at the same time, but they don't. The maturity comes later. You don't realize all the time that you are training your mind in a certain way. Only when you face a test do you understand.

Being sick in the wilderness was a test of my mind and body and I found out I was prepared for it. There are a lot of things the games prepare you for. If I hadn't been that strong I would have been very badly off. I could have ended up as a polar bear dinner.

Chapter 16

The first time I traveled to the World Eskimo-Indian Olympics was in 1978 and I think they took notice of me. I won the Eskimo stick pull, the Indian stick pull, and arm pull. I dominated those events right away. And I took a silver medal in the four-man carry.

By this time I was twenty-five years old, was fully grown to my height of six-foot-four and weighed about three-hundred-and-fifty pounds. People didn't know Eskimos grew that big. I was a big monster.

I had heard about WEIO long before, but either was too busy doing things like school or work, or couldn't afford to fly to Fairbanks. You can't drive from Barrow to anyplace and Fairbanks is four hundred miles south of us, so a jet plane is the only way to go. The Games have been held in Fairbanks, kind of a central location for the big cities and the Bush communities, since they began in the early 1960s. They are held every July in the Big Dipper Ice Arena in the heart of the city during the Golden Days Festival, though they used to be held at the University of Alaska Fairbanks.

One year I went to Fairbanks just to watch and see what the Games were about. I liked what I saw and decided I would come back and compete, so I did, and it's been a big part of my life ever since.

If you watch any other sporting event in the world, whether it is basketball, football, baseball or boxing, you will not see the kind of sportsmanship that you will see during the games. The spirit of the games is unmatched anywhere else. People want to win, but they are always sharing their knowledge and techniques with the other competitors. The idea is to do your best and help others bring out the best in themselves.

That is why you will see someone like Brian Randazzo, who is the best in the world at the two-foot high kick, always stepping up and helping the other competitors when they try their kicks and miss. They are trying to beat him and he will still help them. Before their last try he will be up there putting his arm around them, telling them that they are missing only by a couple of inches and showing them how they can correct it.

You will see that kind of sportsmanship all the time. That is one special thing about the games. Everyone knows the games belong to everybody and it's most important to get the most out of yourself.

It's always exciting to see other athletes give things a try, especially when they haven't tried a game before. And I always find it exciting to tell young athletes how the games originated. They may not be Inupiat Eskimos. They may be Tlingit or Haida or Athabascans and the origins of the games might be new to them. They may never hunt seals or spend time in Barrow in the wintertime. But the games can teach them to survive in their own worlds. They can adapt it. They will have the same instinct to react. They will prove their endurance and test their pain threshold. The basic teachings translate to everyone. Think fast, stay calm, endure.

This is true of people who live in a place like Anchorage, a city of 250,000 people. They do not hunt or fish for subsistence, they may not get caught out in the wild in the winter. But there are driving forces in our lives no matter where we live. All of this training can be useful wherever you live. Life and death situations might occur in the city as well as on the ice. It may take those kind of survival instincts just to get through the day.

Maybe because they don't grow up with the games and the skills the games represent as part of daily life, urban Natives might not come to competition naturally. Brian Randazzo, a good friend, is from Anchorage and he has dominated the two-foot high kick event for more than ten years. But Brian told me he came to the games by chance. Greg Nothstine, another friend of ours, urged him to try it so he did.

Brian admitted he felt a lot of peer pressure in high school to do things that were not necessarily the smartest choices. He found out right away he was good at the games. He has won the Howard Rock Award as the most outstanding athlete at WEIO more than once. He was only sixteen when he started and back then he seemed like he was puffed up with pride. I was, too, at first.

Then I told Brian all the stories behind the games and why we do them the way we do. I told him how the background was passed down to me and when it was I became more humble. I started getting humble as I got older and so did Brian. He was so impressed with the history. Brian is Aleut, his heritage is from the people who come from the Aleutian Islands. That's a place with very different weather than up north. But when I told him about the high kick, I told him, "That's your culture. Stick to it."

The games are more than just a sporting event. They are many things and I try to convey that every way I can.

My first impression of World Eskimo-Indian Olympics as a spectator was a strong one. Just to see all those Native people together, sharing, experiencing things as one, did a lot for me. I didn't even know there were so many different kinds of cultures until I got there. That's what made me want to come back and be part of it. I got some other people together the next year and we all went down.

The Indian stick pull was very new to me.

This is a one-on-one competition. You sit facing each other with your legs crossing each other's. The stick is shorter than the one used in the Eskimo stick pull. In the Indian stick pull the stick is about a foot long and it is tapered at the ends. Then the stick is lathered with grease. I heard in the old days they soaked the stick in a mixture of algae and seal oil and bear grease. Now we use Crisco. The same stuff you use to cook.

Then you grab the stick with one hand, right hand against right hand, or left hand against left hand, and pull.

The Eskimo stick pull involves brute strength. The Indian stick pull is mostly about grip, having strong hands. The background story behind the game is the need to hang on to a fish. I learned that the Indians who lived in the woods who had nothing to fish with could go to the stream and catch fish with their bare hands. They would slowly creep up to the water, reach in, and grab one, hold tight and never let it go. They would let the fish swim by until the tail was passing, then grab it and pull it out of the water. Of course that fish is very slippery. You must have a very strong grip or it will get away.

This game came from the Athabascan Indians. Grab onto the stick and don't let go. It was a different game for me, but I learned I was good at it.

I was the champion who won the gold medal nine years in a row, I think, but then Greg Nothstine beat me. He is much smaller than I am, so it surprised people. Greg kept bugging me, "How do you do it? What is your technique?"

He figured out the key was more about technique than plain strength. I teased him that he could actually beat me if he knew the right way to do it. He kept on bugging me. For a long time I gave him the string and let him hang out to dry.

Finally, I gave in. I showed him. The secret is simple. What you do is grab the stick by the palm of your hand when it is very dry. You don't let any air in there. No moisture. Sure enough, he yanked it right out of my hand.

I won the Eskimo stick pull for ten years in a row and I didn't expect anyone would beat me at that.

Then in 1989, my last year of competition, when I had announced my retirement, Brian Walker of Anchorage came along and defeated me. Big surprise to me. I thought I was going to retire undefeated. But Big Brian beat Big Bob. Brian is pretty big, even if he's not as big as I am, but even though he lives in Anchorage he's strong from commercial fishing in the Bush in the summer.

The four-man carry became one of my best events, too, even if I didn't win it the first year. I was a natural at that because of my size. You would think the world's largest Eskimo should be able to carry six hundred pounds farther than anyone else. Eventually, I did get the record, carrying four men one-hundred-and-ninety-two feet. I had it for a short while. This is one event where you supply all the power. You lift the men off the ground and then you try to put one foot in front of the other as long as you can. You can't go very far, trust me.

This is not a good event for someone who has weak knees. As I got older, my knees started to bother me, so I gave up the four-man carry before I gave up the stick pulls.

By the time I made it to WEIO the first time I was a veteran of Native games competition and I knew where the games came from. So right from the beginning I talked about their history to everyone I met. I had just met Sheila Seetomona who became a good friend and later married Brian Randazzo and she seemed to be impressed with the wisdom I was bringing out. But it was not my wisdom, it was the wisdom of my elders.

I just had great pride in what we were doing and I wanted others to feel that pride, too. It was not as if I had studied this somewhere, it was what I had learned over the years from my father and uncles and my grandpa.

You might expect that people would be surprised someone would come in and start to win right away, but some of the competitors remembered me from Native Youth Olympics, and of course my size kind of impressed them. I think they expected me to be pretty strong.

It would have been easy to be boastful then, but even at the moment I was crowned a world champion I never thought very much about being the best in the world. I thought only of how I had done well by my elders and ancestors. Give all the glory to the ones who came before you, not to yourself. It was the gentle ways of my grandpa and my father who never raised his hand to me that helped make me what I was.

I was taught from the time I was a teenager not to be boastful and that stuck with me. It's good to keep a humble spirit. When you start to see boasting it turns ugly very quickly. Boasting is ugly, ugly, ugly. When you see it, you just know it's not right. Our elders teach that you should be humble when you win and gracious when you lose. If you act otherwise, it is showing disrespect. It's exactly like when my grandpa used to say of inappropriate behavior, "That's not right!"

The spirit of cooperation that I talked about is one of the most critical parts of proper behavior. Although the World Eskimo-Indian Olympics is a good event and I have appreciated being part of it all these years, I believe the elders never really meant for the Games to be competitive at all with the awarding of medals and such. That is not what they are really about.

That's especially true of Eskimo dances. They do give medals for the competitions and whole communities are very proud of that. But the purpose of each dance is to tell a story. The dances were always about storytelling and sharing of knowledge.

When you watch Eskimo dancing, you see people of all ages, from the very young to the very old, moving in unison and in rhythm to the beat of the drums. The drums are the heartbeat of the message. You watch the hands show the motions of the birds or animals in the story and the way feet are stomped. And the words of the stories are never sung in English, only in Inupiaq.

Eskimo dancing is pure joy, our way of expressing ourselves. I remember one old man was out on the sea ice one time. He came to the edge of the ice and started dancing right in front of the whale. Really getting down, too. He looked completely overjoyed. I was thinking, "What in the world is he doing?" I didn't realize at first that he was just expressing sheer joy for the fact that the Creator would give us such bounty. He was thankful we would have this great whale to eat. I was young at the time and I didn't think of his reasons for many years. That's maturity showing up. It takes a long time to understand such things. It's a process.

There are only a few places where the Native games are contested regularly. The other highlight event for us as adults, once we are too old for NYO, is called the Arctic Winter Games. The Arctic Winter Games is an Olympics of the north. Alaska competes against teams from the Yukon Territory, the Northwest Territories and other places in Canada. These events are held every two years in March and involve many other sports, like hockey and skiing, too.

I have been to several Arctic Winter Games all over the north as an athlete and a coach and I always have a good time. You spend a week in dormitories with your friends and competitors. In 1994, when the event was held in Slave Lake, Northwest Territories, I was coaching.

When we arrived in this very small place, I rented a car. But there was something wrong with it and I wanted to return it. They didn't have any more available, so the owner lent me his car. It was a big Chevrolet convertible.

By Barrow standards it wasn't very cold out, maybe thirty degrees or so. So I put the top down. I thought, Why not? It took me a little while to get it down. I was the driver, but I was with Brian Randazzo and Brian Walker and a couple of other guys and we drove around town like that. Everybody was looking at us. I could hear them talking. They were thinking, Who is this nut?

We had that car for almost a whole week. I did put the top up when it started raining, but the sun was out most of the time. The girls were looking at us. We were waving and they would wave back. It finally did get too cold to drive around like that and I put it back up. Us Alaskans just figured it was summer. We were good old boys driving around who didn't want to bother with the shuttle bus.

We had a good time at the Arctic Winter Games that year.

When I first went to the World Eskimo-Indian Olympics, I was not just trying to win, I was trying to dominate, but I never felt puffed up by what I was doing. There is a difference between enjoying what you have accomplished and being arrogant and boastful about it. If you know you are the best, there is some pleasure to be gained from that, but I thought of my uncle. He was the best at games in Barrow, but he never looked down on others whom he'd beaten. He never said he was the best. That is for others to say, not yourself. He knew he was the best, but he didn't have to say it. Humble is the way to be. Whatever happens, happens. Like it comes out of heaven when you win.

I got satisfaction out of winning the events and winning the gold medals. I don't want to pretend that I didn't. But I took the medals off pretty quickly. I gave some away to kids, but I still have others on a string hanging in my bedroom at home in Barrow. I am proud.

I am prouder, though, of my role in becoming a teacher to the next generation of athletes. Like Brian Randazzo. He is becoming a teacher himself. I trained him and I expect him to be training someone else now that he is in his thirties. As good as Brian was at the high kick, he is stronger mentally. He is good inside, where it counts.

Brian showed how strong he is in an important way and how much he gained from the Games when he got seriously hurt at the Arctic Winter Games competition in the Northwest Territories in 1994. He hurt his knee badly and had to be flown to a hospital. Many people said he was all through and would never be the same again.

Brian worked so hard and he came back to the Arctic Winter Games when they were held in Chugiak, Alaska two years later. And he won the gold medal again. That was the survival training that enabled him to do that. I was right there when he won. I was very happy to see it.

Chapter 17

Although most of the games we play at the World Eskimo-Indian Olympics have special meaning behind them, we do play some games just for fun. They were invented by watching animals in the wild.

There was one game I learned as a young man that was like having a bullfight on your knees. You go shoulder-to-shoulder like two caribou butting each other. I think that game originated when people watched big caribou fighting during the rutting season.

The neck pull had its origin in a way that is not too romantic. But it evolved from subsistence hunting. Sometimes two adult seals battle over a dead seal pup. Pups get killed when seals go to mate sometimes and then there was a tug of war over the dead pup.

All of the high-kick events, the two-foot high kick, and the one-foot high kick, test quick thinking and quick reflexes when the jumper leaps up, leaving his feet, to kick a dangling fur-covered seal ball. The hopping events got started by hunters who were down on their knees on the ice and sprang to their feet in one motion.

There is a belief in many places that the two-foot high kick represented a signal from the hunters sent back to the people in camp. I have heard it said that the jumping indicated success. But that's just a myth. I've heard it said many times, but I've never heard that from the elders.

The blanket toss is just a part of celebrations. The blanket toss is always a crowd pleaser. We have blanket tosses in Barrow outdoors in the spring at the end of the whaling season. I think when the whalers came home they invited the whole community to celebrate with them. I don't know how old it is. Ancient. The blanket toss is not a signal for anything the way some people think, either. It's just for fun.

We also have the blanket toss indoors at WEIO. The Big Dipper Arena, the site of the Games, is basically a two-story hockey rink with a mirrored ceiling that has seats for more than two thousand people. The competitors in the blanket toss take it as a great challenge to try to touch the ceiling and even push aside one of the glass panels. I have seen them do it.

The blanket is from the ugruk, sealskin cloth with ropes attached to the edges. You need forty or more "pullers" who stretch the sealskin taut. Then when they flip the blanket up and down, it makes a whooshing noise. It gives the competitor some spring to fly through the air. No competitor can get good height if the pullers are out of synch. I usually help organize the pullers. I guess I am a good puller because I am in demand. I energize that thing.

You should try the blanket toss if you get the chance because it is fun, but you should not eat a heavy meal right before you get on the blanket. Bad things can happen to your stomach. You might get airsick.

My absolute favorite game is one that is not part of the Native Youth Olympics or WEIO, but we played it at the Christmas Games in Barrow. It's called the laughing game. People form a circle, and we toss a really light handkerchief or scarf into the air. As long as that handkerchief is suspended in the air and is coming down, we all have to keep laughing really hard. Until it hits the floor or somebody grabs it out of the air. And then suddenly you must stop laughing. You can't even smile. You can't show any emotion. Whoever smiles or blurts out a laugh is out of the game.

That's one game I really liked, but I wasn't too good at it. I laughed too easily.

Probably my favorite game of all those contested at WEIO is the four-man carry. It just thrills me to see some little guy come along and do well. Of course, to me just about everyone else is a little guy. But someone like my friends Homer Lord or Chris Benson, they are powerful, but they're not really tall and not very heavy. But they have the strength to do well.

The four-man carry looks hard to everyone and so that scares some people off right away. The hardest part is getting started. When the four people climb on, you have to bend your knees to lift them up. Once they are up on you, walking isn't as hard as long as you keep breathing in and out deeply. A lot of times you're straining all your muscles and you forget to breathe. Then you get in trouble. As long as you're breathing, you're okay, but it's hard to do.

I never have packed seals like that, but I have carried a whole caribou home across my shoulders. I gutted it first, then carried it. The mosquitoes were getting so bad, I didn't want to sit there and finish, so I grabbed the thing and walked to the boat. It weighed two hundred pounds, but I carried it a lot farther than my WEIO record of one-hundred-and-ninety-two feet.

After you stop in the four-man carry, it's a very strange feeling. You feel like your whole body is going to float right up in the air the moment they get off. You have such a light feeling, a feeling that you're going to hit the ceiling. It's instant relief. But a little while later you start to feel the pain. Your knees start hurting, and your back. Several years after I retired, I attempted the four-man carry at WEIO for old times' sake. But I just couldn't do it anymore. My knees and back hurt right away. Ugh, too much.

In 1989, when I decided to retire from active competition, people didn't believe me. I was feeling my age in my bones, but I also thought maybe people were starting to think we needed new champions in some events. I thought about it for a while. We did need new faces. It was time to give others a turn in the Indian stick pull and the Eskimo stick pull.

For a long time I had been there to take all the awards and stuff and I think competitors were getting discouraged. I just thought it was time for the younger ones to get an opportunity. I started to notice some younger athletes wouldn't participate. When it gets to be too one-sided people don't want to participate.

I told everybody I really was going to retire. I always thought that I would come back and be an official, but I wanted the kids to take over the events. As it turned out, I got beat in the Indian stick pull and the Eskimo stick pull anyway. I was going out at just the right time.

When Brian Walker came along and beat me in the Eskimo stick pull I was really surprised, though I knew he could give me a run for my money. He yanked that stick away from me. I figured I would go out on top, but he came along and fooled me.

The next year, 1990, I didn't go to WEIO. Everybody thought I would, but when July rolled around I was out boating. I didn't even realize the dates passed until I saw my relatives who came home from the games and told me they missed me there in Fairbanks.

I thought it was time to leave the games — it was interfering a little bit with my subsistence hunting — but I got invited back as an official and I thought I would try that. So I've been going back every year since to help out.

Then once, during a slow time, I just got on the microphone and started talking to the crowd as a commentator. It just happened. It wasn't planned. And then

I had a new job. Information please!

I looked around the Big Dipper and I saw maybe two thousand fans watching, but I didn't have the sense that they were paying attention the whole time or knew what they were watching. They came because they wanted to see something new and different, but no one was telling people exactly what it was all about. They wanted to be educated, and we wanted them to be educated and I just thought I would try to do it. Many of those visitors were tourists new to Alaska who would only see the games once in their lives. I wanted them to take something home with them they would remember — and understand.

So I started talking.

I introduce myself as the world's largest Eskimo and that makes people take a look. Then I tell a few jokes to get their attention. Sometimes I talk with a Texas-type accent. And sometimes I talk with a deep, deep voice, like my uncle's intimidating voice. So here you have the world's largest Eskimo talking to them and speaking with a funny accent. That works. One day there will be a scout for The Tonight Show with Jay Leno and he will sign me up. For later, after I retire from my job.

I got my inspiration from Al Grant who used to talk on the microphone at the games. That guy was so funny. Everybody would be laughing all the time. Not a boring moment. And when it wouldn't get quiet for the competitors, he'd just step right up there and say, "Shut up! They're trying to kick!" I think that was the only time there was quiet.

Telling the jokes has a purpose, though. If I don't have the fans' attention I am just talking into the air. My voice is not connecting with them. But when I know they're listening, I can slip in some history.

I don't have an act or a routine. Every time I get on the microphone I am ad-libbing. It just comes out thought by thought when I'm out there. I hope I can think of something funny to say.

One time I remember in my last year of competing in the Eskimo stick pull the luck of the draw put me up against Boogles Johnson. He was only twelve years old and a wee little fellow. I could sit there and hold the stick with one hand and wave to the crowd with the other hand while he struggled away, pulling at that stick. Of course, he couldn't move me. Afterwards he gave me a big hug. The crowd enjoyed that and it gave me the idea that I might be able to make people laugh.

Another time, after I retired, a young newcomer was doing real well in the Eskimo stick pull. He was a big guy, too. And I just blurted out on the microphone, "He reminds me of me." Everybody laughed at that one. That was Solomon Elook. It just came out. I started calling him King Solomon. I wanted to crown him. Then when he won I told everybody he would have to go up against me. It was just a silly thing to do, to get people talking and keep up the interest.

If people are listening to the jokes, they will be listening to the background of the games. What I want the audience to know is why we do these amazing looking games, what the history is that shows they are more than just games, and to learn about the climate we come from.

It might be eighty or ninety degrees in Fairbanks during the Games. The spectators might be wearing short sleeves. I want them to understand the harsh, unforgiving nature of where we live and how in Barrow in the middle of the summer it won't be eighty degrees, it actually might snow.

I also want them to know that when they are looking at Eskimo dancers, it is not just a dance, but a story about a way of life. Most of the dance leaders don't speak English, so the spectators don't know what they're seeing, they don't know that the dancers are acting out real things from the old days.

Sometimes when an athlete like Brian Randazzo is doing the high kick, I will say, "You are watching the best in the world." I say it real quietly and that perks people up. For someone who has never seen the two-foot high kick, it puts it in perspective.

The reason I grabbed the microphone the first time was that I saw some people tuning it all out, yawning. A lot of times when you are out on the floor, getting ready for an event, you look around at the stands and see what people are doing. I would do anything to get people interested. I might see these cute tourist girls and start teasing them.

I always enjoy being at the games, no matter how I am involved. I think making jokes helps everyone, even the athletes. They are on the edge, waiting to compete and they have butterflies. If they don't start relaxing before their event, they might completely miss. I used to tell Brian that he was too tense. I would sit him down and tell him to relax. Sometimes he would miss his first two tries, but for his third attempt he would kick good because he would be relaxed. He wouldn't feel the pressure.

Sometimes I do miss competing, so I enter the Christmas Games. I still do the Eskimo stick pull. Once in a while in Barrow, I see some of the younger athletes really getting boastful and hollering. I'll get all riled up and just step up there to show them. Sometimes I'll just step forward and issue a challenge and no one will take it. If you have issued a challenge, and a count of ten seconds passes and nobody responds, you win.

I try not to dwell on being out of competition. I try to replace it with my involvement in subsistence hunting. It's hard, but I do my best to put it out of my mind. If you let yourself think about it for a little while, soon enough you are thinking about it a lot and it just gets to you. If I'm hunting, going after ugruk, it's easy to forget. If I'm out boating, it's easy to forget. I love boating.

Once in a while when I am back at WEIO as an official or am working on the microphone I think about how it would be for me to jump into one event. If I felt I had to charge up the crowd, I would. But I don't really want to do it. I'm retired. I'm finished with it. I had my time. If I did one event, I'd probably just be kidding.

I spend more of my time involvement with the games as an official during the events and as a member of the board of directors year-round. By 1995 I was vice-president and when the president stepped aside because of job commitments I ended up as president for the last four months of her term.

Being on the board you don't get paid. You are a volunteer. What does being president of WEIO mean to me? It's an honor, but it brings a lot of headaches. It did seem amazing that all of this time passed since I first went to compete in the Games and all of a sudden I was president of the whole organization.

But I don't dwell on that. I just do all I can to improve the events and preserve the traditions. It's an opportunity to do what I can to keep the games in line with the teachings of the elders.

I am also a district-wide coordinator for Native Youth Olympics and I coordinate all the events in Barrow. I bring in all the kids from the villages. Directly after that in April I take a bunch of kids to Anchorage to compete statewide. These kids are ages eleven and older, up to eighteen.

I always enjoy working with the kids. For a lot of them, this is their first exposure to the games. To me that's a fresh audience. You turn me loose and I will tell everyone about the history. I also encourage them individually. If they didn't do well one time I tell them never to give up. There's always another year.

Part of what I tell them is to always have fun. There is a lot of activity going on, and competition, but especially when we go to Anchorage, to a bigger city when all the other competitors are there from around the state, they should have fun.

I also lay down my first law — don't rile me. There are strict rules for the road trip. If they don't behave, they know they will be sent home. I don't preach to them about what I did when I was their age, or tell them much about what I did when I competed in the games. I expect them to behave and practice.

Many of them know who I am and respect me, anyway, but they are thinking more about what they are doing than what I did. A lot of times when they are feeling down, perhaps just after they lost an event, I will go over and put an arm around them to cheer them up. I talk to them, I motivate them.

Sometimes that's a good time to be me, when size makes a difference. I would do what my elders would do to encourage them. I tell them how proud of them I am and I tell them they were going up against the best in the state. I think that demands respect once they know how far you've gone.

They seem to listen to me because they know I talk about respect a lot and how important it is. Not only for the elders, but also for themselves and the people and things around them.

And I try to live that way. I think the best way to give an example to the kids is to show them by being a good example. Actions speak louder than words and when they see that, it helps. I do a lot more acting than speaking.

Sometimes hugging counts just as much, just letting them know that you care. It's comforting combining words with action, action with words.

I talk about the role of elders a lot and, of course, most people think elders are really, really old. In most instances, the oldest people have the most wisdom because they have been around for a long time accumulating it.

Life experience counts. Learning from mistakes and past experience, but that isn't all of it. A twenty-year-old man could be an elder based on what he's been through and how he has acted. Or a forty-year-old woman. Really, anybody who is older than you who passes on wisdom can be considered an elder and is deserving of your respect.

I would not say that I am an elder. I am still learning. People don't really call themselves elders. Others call them elders. I would never tell anybody that I am an elder. I would feel unworthy of that at this point in my life. I am a coach, and I teach and dispense wisdom to younger people, but that doesn't make me an elder by itself.

I may be somone who delivers information, but I think of elders as wise people. I just try to set a good example in what I do and how I live, to act as a protector of the knowledge handed down through the ages. In the long run, it will benefit young people the way it benefited me.

Chapter 18

After I went away to high school for a little while and then had my job training in Montana, I came back to Barrow and stayed for good.

Almost my whole adult life I have worked driving heavy machinery up and down the roads of Barrow, smoothing the roads out. The thing I like best about my job is that I know I am providing a service for the community.

When I hear people say the roads are smooth and somebody calls into our maintenance office at the headquarters and compliments us or the whole operation, it makes me feel good. That means we are doing something good, something right, and it's all for the community. And I think everyone in Barrow knows it.

It makes me feel that I am an essential part of the community. It's satisfying to know that you moved a mountain of dirt or snow. Every winter we move mountains of snow. There's satisfaction in that, and of staying on top of it and having the whole community be impressed and very appreciative. Little stuff like that goes a long, long way. You know you're doing honest work.

I often work from seven o'clock in the morning until past three o'clock in the afternoon for the North Slope Borough, but the hours can vary. Sometimes I work on weekends, too, and sometimes I get called in when they need me, like after a snowstorm. I have never figured out how many miles a day I drive, but I bet in the course of the year it's thousands and thousands of miles in a pretty small place.

I sit up high in the catbird seat in my glassed-in cab, rumbling through the streets on the big yellow grader all day long. People wave. They say, "There goes Big Bob. Watch out!" And I wave back. It's fun. I'll tell you, the grader is one big vehicle. It's about as long as a brontosaurus. It's not something you can parallel park just anywhere like a car in the city.

Even though I am only in my mid-forties, I have been operating heavy equipment for about two-thirds of my life, full-time for just over twenty years. But even before I got the full training courses, I had experience with heavy equipment. When I was still a teenager I worked in the summer doing jobs that required driving trucks and using heavy equipment.

I have always enjoyed moving mountains. From an early age I thought it was the right thing for me. My destiny was to operate heavy equipment. My profession is a good fit. Maybe it makes sense that I drive big machines. The world's largest Eskimo moves the earth with the world's largest machines. Well, that's not exactly true, but it feels like it.

When I was a little boy and rode around with my dad I got the idea I would want to drive heavy equipment when I grew up and I was right. I like the feeling of moving mountains and I like driving in general. Maybe if I had been born and grew up in the lower forty-eight states I would have been a long distance truck driver. Up in Barrow, though, we don't have many roads at all. The farthest you can go is twelve miles out of town to Point Barrow. You can't go out of town much of anywhere else. All of the other roads are inside the city of 4,100 people, through the neighborhoods, to the airport.

I drive up and down those roads all the time and I like being able to spend my time behind the wheel. Sitting high in the cab you get a pretty good view of everything. You can watch the dirt moving, the earth being turned. Sometimes it feels like you can see the whole world from up there.

Over the years, I have been a volunteer firefighter for the community, and handled administration of the borough Native Youth Olympics. I belong to a traditional games committee and I officiate a lot during the Christmas Games. And I've become involved fully with The Inupiat Assembly of God.

After all of my years driving heavy equipment, there came a time in the early 1990s when I was intrigued by an offer to try another line of work. In 1994, I got the opportunity to become recreation director for the city of Barrow. I parked my trucks for a while, so to speak.

I became the overseer of all the recreation programs in Barrow and supervised about nine employees. It was my job to make things happen.

I was very excited about this. It gave me a chance to put together activities, festivals, and other recreation for our young people, as well as the adults, and to help improve the playgrounds.

At the time, in 1994 and 1995, there was a lot of debate going on about whether Barrow would be a dry town — no alcohol — or be a damp town, a place where you can bring it home for yourself. Some people who relied on alcohol a lot complained there would be nothing to do. I had it in my head to make sure there were activities for everyone so there would always be something to do.

It's not good when people just sit around. Especially kids. So I tried to get new programs going.

The mayor called to me and asked me if I would try this new job and it appealed to me for two very important reasons. I wanted to do something for the kids and I wanted to do something for the elderly people. Being recreation director totally involved both of them. I especially wanted to do some work that would keep the kids around me.

I felt I would be in a position to give advice and affect kids' lives at a critical time when they would make choices. I hoped I could influence them to make the right choices and I hoped I could provide them with some things to do, too.

We started a little dribbler's basketball league and started up Little League baseball. All kinds of things like that. The programs started to get pretty successful. After that we started up a basketball league and a softball association for adults and got directly involved in all the recreation activities around town.

I enjoyed what I was doing very much. I loved it. But the job only lasted two years. There was a new administration in the government and a lot of people changed over. I was asked to stay, but I felt as if my time was up, that I'd done my part. It sounded as if they were expecting too much of me. It was time to move on and right then there was an opening back at my old place with the North Slope Borough. So I went back to driving heavy equipment.

I went back to moving mountains. And it still is a very satisfying job for me.

Chapter 19

After all of my early years of competing in the Native Youth Olympics and the World Eskimo-Indian Olympics in Alaska, I was given some chances to demonstrate Native sports in other parts of the country. I was excited by the idea of the travel and also excited to have the opportunity to educate people about our way of life.

The most spectacular appearance I ever made was as coordinator of the group that went from Alaska to demonstrate at the Summer Olympics in Los Angeles in 1984. We demonstrated the Native sports for the athletes who had come from all over the world.

About eight of us got to go, including Brian and Sheila Randazzo, Joshua Okpik from Barrow and Reggie Joule from Kotzebue. Reggie is one of the greatest Native athletes of all time. He won medals in so many events I couldn't count them. One of his best events was the blanket toss and I think he even got to do it on national television once. Also, the Wainwright dancers went because they were the number one dance group that year. ARCO, the oil company, paid our expenses as a sponsor. We were selected by WEIO officials as the ones to go to Los Angeles to introduce our culture to the world.

We named ourselves The Heartbeats of Alaska. It was not a name that we had before, but we sat around and discussed it and came up with that name, which was very popular. The name came from the Eskimo drum. When we were talking we were trying to come up with something that represented us all. Every time you beat the drum it sounds like a heartbeat. We all lined up ready to go for it when we thought it up.

The drum gives out a certain tone. This is our beat. It comes from the heart. Okay, we thought, "How about the Heartbeats?" It just evolved. We got started talking, throwing ideas out and said, "How about Heartbeats of Alaska?" Someone said, "Hey, that doesn't sound too bad." We decided it was a good name. Our drums make a sound and the drums we beat come from the heart with joy. It's the expression of our lives and the power that goes out, an echo. The more we talked about it, the more we thought it was a real good name because our emblem was a drum. Everyone always remembers that name.

Right after Los Angeles, we went on to Washington, D.C. We were there in July for about ten days. Man, that was hot. Every day we did demonstrations at the fairgrounds by the Lincoln Memorial. There was a festival going on with people from all over the world and the government invited us to participate. I got the chance to demonstrate the four-man carry, the Eskimo stick pull, the finger pull and other strength events.

I'll never forget how hot it was. Washington in the summertime is about as different from Barrow as you can get. For one thing, it gets dark. Just kidding. The temperatures got up into the nineties and there was humidity that made you sweat all the time. We don't have any humidity in Barrow.

The people were nice, though. I had already been to Washington, D.C. for a similar event when I was in high school, and the people were just about the same. They were interested in what we were doing and enthusiastic. But they still asked some pretty ridiculous questions.

Once again everyone seemed to ask if we were living in igloos. They still thought that. That came up all the time. I bet we were asked that at least ten times a day. When there was a break one time we were joking among ourselves and said maybe we should just start telling everyone that we do live in igloos. That would blow their minds. The temptation was strong.

I did it one time. Just said it with a straight face. "Of course we live in igloos." They believed me. I couldn't help but chuckle. At one point, I started thinking I should say "I'm a full-blooded Inupiat and if you don't back off, I will eat you." But I never did that.

I guess I thought people from other parts of the country would be better informed about us than they were. But then, sometimes I think just as many people who live in Alaska are not informed about Eskimos. They seem to have many silly ideas. I run into people in Anchorage and they don't know anything about

Native customs. That shouldn't be the case if they live in Alaska. Maybe those people I met in Alaska were just passing through.

You might say that summer I traveled I was just carrying on the family tradition. My parents, Robert and Martha, have been members of the Barrow dance group for a long time and they have danced all over the place. They not only made appearances all over the country, they've been to Korea and to St. Petersburg, Russia. While they were spreading our culture to other places, they got a chance to see other cultures in other places as part of their experience.

During the summer of 1984 I spent a lot of time demonstrating Native sports in the lower forty-eight and it was mostly a good experience. But I have also done a lot more demonstrations for television crews over the years. I do try to always get the message across about World Eskimo-Indian Olympics and the history of our games. That's a constant thing with me.

I have been on television all over the world. I can't even remember how many film crews from how many different countries have filmed us. All over the lower forty-eight for starters. But also crews from Sweden, Japan and other places. I know there was a documentary of the World Eskimo-Indian Olympics made more than once. There was one from Australia. We had people in Fairbanks from ESPN. I know there was a newspaper article about me in a Swedish newspaper. And I saw one from Japan and one from Australia.

I once had three Navajo Indians come up to me and say, "Hi, Big Bob." And I didn't recognize them. So I asked them, "How do you know me?" And they said, "We saw you on TV." So that's how I know I've been on TV in a lot of places.

Certainly, the story of the athletes and the World Eskimo-Indian Olympics has been spread across many lands. Big Bob's moccasins have gone far. Or — let me rephrase that — my mukluks have gone far. At least on video tape.

Chapter 20

Barrow is the land of cold. To most people it is unimaginable how cold Barrow can be. It can be about twenty degrees below zero most of the winter.

And that doesn't feel cold to me. I am used to it.

Winter as a season really starts in the fall on the calendar. Often, we get blowing snow in November. It might snow a lot in the fall. And we might not get more snow for a while. Whatever comes down, though, stays. It doesn't melt. About the coldest I remember it getting on the thermometer is about sixty or seventy degrees below zero. But since we get a lot of wind pretty regularly, the windchill can be eighty-five or a hundred degrees below zero. Man, that is cold.

I don't like the wind. The wind is our enemy. It can be twenty below and be very pretty outside. Blue sky. Beautiful scenery. But that wind, man, it will cut you to the bone.

The coldest weather comes in late January and early February, right when the sun comes up for the year. It will be bright, but clear. The temperature might shoot down to around fifty below. That's more than average cold.

People think Eskimos never get cold, but Barrow even gets cold for us. It happens. Twenty below is not a big deal. Thirty below, I might not be out snowmachining, but that would be the only difference in daily life for me. Forty below, I stay at home.

That's the cutoff. At forty below I don't do much. Nobody does much. We're not out on the ice. We're not out hunting. At fifty below you will have some pipes in homes and buildings start to freeze up, though we're well-equipped now to face the winter because of technology and Eskimo ingenuity.

If it gets to sixty below, I turn on the TV set, lock the door and throw the phone off the hook. Let your fingers do the walking. Wise men say, Don't move.

The coldest temperature I ever lived through was seventy below zero. But the funny thing is, it was in Fairbanks, not Barrow. It was during high school. There were no winds. It was just dead air. Cold, dead air. Imagine that, Fairbanks colder than Barrow. That would fool some people, I bet.

As I said, we are well-equipped for the cold. Barrow is a pretty modern town compared to most villages in the Alaska Bush. We have an airport, hotels, restaurants, a sophisticated water system. Maybe it's not modern compared to New York, but compared to most places. That wasn't always true, though. Technology has changed a lot in my lifetime and it has vastly improved our lifestyle.

When I was a youngster, about ten years old, my brothers and I used to get up in the middle of the night, taking turns, to light the stove with driftwood. When we woke up there would be frost on the inside of the walls and the ceiling of the house. We'd jump out of bed real quick and light the stove and then jump right back into bed. It was never what you would call toasty in our house in the winter months.

Then we converted to coal heating. The coal would burn into the night, but sometime in the middle of the night while we were sleeping it would go out, and we were back where we were before. To make up for that, we had a good wood stove right next to the coal stove. Two stoves. I remember going through that. I remember it seemed like we were always gathering wood in those days.

After using coal, our Native corporation shipped in stove oil from Seattle for us and we started using that, but it made the house stink. Eventually they found the natural gas and developed the fields and we use that now. It eliminated stove oil. We kept the wood stoves, though, for backup to take to our fish camps.

Overall, in many ways, life has gotten easier since I was a kid. Definitely. I remember using dog teams and then I remember snowmachines just coming on the scene. My dad bought a snowmachine and we were just fooling around with it, but before I turned around, snowmachines had eliminated dog teams. I don't miss the dogs.

And then all these vehicles started appearing in the streets. They were brought in by barge, or some of them were flown in. Cars and trucks and buses. Visitors are surprised to see city buses. They are top-of-the-line equipment. It's because of oil money that we have them.

The Alaska Native Claims Settlement Act gave millions of acres of land to

Natives all over Alaska to make up for past injustices and it also gave Native corporations millions of dollars. Well, it turned out that the Prudhoe Bay oil field was on Native land and we could tax them. That helped make the North Slope Borough one of the richest places around. It changed everything that way. Oil made a tremendous difference from the 1970s on, especially after the eight-hundred-mile Alaska Pipeline was built from Prudhoe Bay to Valdez.

Most people went from total subsistence living to being dependent on a paycheck. Technology struck and the population grew. When my dad got married about fifty years ago, he said there were maybe only four hundred people in Barrow. I know there were only about a thousand for a long time and now there's at least four times that many.

Until the oil activity, there weren't that many people here. Oil made for a big boom, a big boom in money here. A lot of people who work for the borough government make more than $100,000 a year. In the early 1980s, they built a high school for about $70 million. It was the most expensive high school in the world at the time. It still might be.

Sometimes I think it was just a big waste of money and if everybody went to Mount Edgecumbe in Sitka they'd be better off. The students still drop out like flies. I think the education in Mount Edgecumbe is better. When you are right at home, there are too many distractions to interfere with studying. One kid, I asked him why he dropped out of school, and he said he was bored. I hear that a lot from a lot of kids. Sometimes technology and fancier buildings aren't the answer.

There is a three-story office building in downtown Barrow. It cost something-millions of dollars to build. There's more substantial, warmer housing than ever. There are more wage-earning jobs and higher wages. Oil money has been a mixed blessing, I think.

It's good in a way. We have satellite television that connects us all over the world. We get television shows from all over the nation, from Canada, from Denver, from Chicago. Now we know what the whole world is like. We know what to expect when we go to other towns or other countries.

We have high-quality computers, too. I remember in the winter the high school kids were talking to people from Africa by satellite. Actually talking to them, answering each other's questions. That is a tremendous change. This is the technology we have now and a window to the world is within our grasp. It's a remarkable change when you think that not so many years ago we didn't have any television at all and had no contact with people from other places outside Alaska.

One thing I worry about is our young people being deprived of a traditional cultural education. With our new schools — we have a new elementary school, too, built a few years ago — education should be better. Should be. I just don't know if the young Eskimos in the modern world are getting the right all-around education. I think when we started educating our children with western culture's programs we might have left out a lot of values. We didn't know how to approach our children and teach them ways that will benefit them in the long run in Barrow. We have just said, "Okay, let's try this and do this." Instead of thinking how to implement and teach our young people to speak Inupiaq.

We may have shiny new buildings, but there are things that are being missed. It bothers me because these are our future leaders.

This could be remedied, but education has become so political. We need to leave the political part alone and start getting down to the nitty-gritty of actually helping younger children to understand and learn the way our culture is.

One reason I say technology is a mixed blessing is because young people get too wrapped up in the new technology. They watch television and play video games and they really must go much farther, learning new things, but also learning old things. We must learn to combine the best of new things and the best of old ways.

Part of it is motivation to do both. That must come from parents, aunts and uncles. The motivation behind each student to excel and learn more is not here within our schools the way it should be. It's a tremendous challenge to combine both worlds.

Of course, this challenge is not brand new. This has been the challenge of the last fifteen or so years. But it is possible to be a fifteen-year-old who watches cable television and also participates in the Native Youth Olympics.

Guidance is needed. Everything points to the family. I think it would be a big motivation for children if their parents were fully involved in their activities, but they're not. That would be the start of a healthier relationship and a healthy education would grow from that.

If there's no encouragement or backup from the family, I can see how education could be boring. The kids are in their own little world of education and they have to go through it themselves.

Sure, some people might say that it is impossible to have the best of both worlds, that we now have jet planes coming to Barrow and satellite television and it's time to let go of the past. Look at me. I got hold of both worlds and I mastered them. I have control.

Not without a struggle. But nothing good comes without a struggle. It was both worlds fighting against each other within me for a while for a long time. I wanted this. I wanted that. I wanted to stay in the Inupiat world. And I wanted to be part of the western world. Both worlds were colliding with each other.

The biggest battle of my life was fighting alcoholism. I made a big mistake drinking, even if I was unhappy back in high school. I had reasons, but there is no excuse. The lessons to do the right thing were right there for me, but I wasn't wise enough or strong enough to take advantage of them.

In the long run the advice of my parents and my grandpa did save me from drinking. When I made myself stop drinking I had people say it took me long enough.

When I was younger I was disgusted with life and bored. But I said to myself, "I'm going to learn as much as I can." Listen, watch and learn. I had motivation from my grandpa and my uncles and some of my friends were motivating me. Some of my teachers told me I had a pretty good head on my shoulders, to use it. I had a lot of good motivators in my life. I had a lot of good friends helping me.

It did not happen overnight, but I do feel I have mastered both worlds. I am still involved with the World Eskimo-Indian Olympics, whaling and subsistence hunting, but I have been to Los Angeles, and Washington, D.C., and Montana and New York, Arizona and Florida.

Existing in both worlds comes at a price, though. It takes a lot of your time and energy. You make a lot of mistakes. You give up a lot. There are a lot of heartaches. You do a lot of thinking and accept challenges. You will be cut down by racists. You might be cut down by your own family because of jealousy. You get cut down by a lot of people with different perspectives. People are sure they know how you should be.

When I was growing up I was so close with my brothers. We were best friends. But then we grew up and went in different ways. We started to make money and I worked hard and I thought they were not as dedicated as me. Sometimes I think we are total strangers living under one roof, or living in one town.

We are at the age now where we recognize our differences and we are trying to share things again and are trying to connect again, but it's not the same. There seems to be a veil between us when we reach out. I could never reach through that. I am closer to my younger brother Percy and my nephews. But there are times I just get frustrated with my relationship with my other brothers. There is some sadness there.

You can't turn the clock back, but sometimes I wish the clock never advanced, that nobody cared about anything except hunting, fishing, the family and the community. The technology has been wonderful and it has been hard.

In my lifetime, I have seen a lot of changes in Barrow. From dog sled to snowmachine. From wood stove to natural gas burning. Technology was abruptly put in front of our faces. Either you go with it, or you are left behind. The choice is limited. Either you master both worlds, or you are left behind.

Chapter 21

Ten feet away. The polar bear crawled up on the ice, dripping water, and slowly climbed to its feet. Ten feet from me.

We were butchering a whale on the ice when the polar bear swam up to us. It was not a huge surprise. Some of us were there acting as guards, with our rifles loaded.

Polar bears are fearsome creatures. Most bears, brown bears and black bears, spend their lives in the woods or mountains and they stay away from people. We don't have woods or mountains near Barrow, but sea ice and tundra. Polar bears do not mingle with people freely, but they have no fear of humans when they are hungry. Most of the time they will not alter their behavior and habits in search of food if men get in the way.

This is especially true if the bear hasn't eaten in a while. And that day, you could tell right away, this polar bear was hungry. He was skinny and looked half-starved. He just came up out of the water, onto the ice and started sniffing around the whale. He wanted dinner. The bear had its nose up in the air, looking around, looking like he just might take a leap at us or the whale.

Polar bears can weigh up to fifteen hundred pounds. They have claws a few inches long and teeth that will give you a scare. Everyone pictures polar bears as a solid white, but their fur reflects the sunlight so when they get up close they can seem more yellowish, or greyish white. The snout is black and the paws are black. They may look cute to some people, but not from ten feet away, that's for sure.

A lot of times a polar bear will choose to avoid man, but not when it comes to a debate over a meal. They don't care who, or what, is in their way. Brown bears or black bears might have experience with people if they live in a national park or close to a populated area. Not so polar bears. The average polar bear will never come into contact with humans. It's a comparatively rare thing. It happens, though, up near Barrow.

A hungry polar bear will attack. They will seriously maim you to get at your whale.

This time, when the bear crawled up on the ice, someone near me fired a few rounds from his rifle into the air, hoping the noise would scare the bear away. Bad idea. It didn't work. The bear stood up and it was about a nine-footer. It just looked at that guy and kept coming closer. I swung around with a slug gun and fired at the bear. Then everybody was shooting at it wildly. But the slugs just weren't penetrating his coat.

The bear was dripping wet. Its hair was soaked from the swim and it made the fur work like armor. I wanted to wait for my best shot until the bear wiggled its body to get rid of all that water. I knew it was coming, but it's hard to be patient in a situation like that. It's all you can do, though.

"Wait till he shakes off the water!" I shouted. Otherwise, it was just a waste of our ammunition. People were shooting at him, anyway, and some of them were hitting him, I know. But with the wet fur the bear might as well have been a tank. The bear just shrugged off the bullets. It was like shooting a dinosaur with a BB gun. We weren't reaching any vital organs with the hits. Even with a .30-06 rifle the bullet only penetrated an inch maybe. It can't stop an enraged bear. That sopping wet fur makes all the difference.

Finally, the bear shook off some water and I had a chance and shot. The slug shell went right through its neck, right below the head, at the base of the skull. It was an accurate shot, but because the bullet went all the way through, it didn't have the full effect. The force did make the bear jump back. The bear staggered, then it stumbled backwards and fell into the water.

I jumped back a step or two. Since I was aiming for the neck and since I expected it to jump forward when I shot, I moved the other way. Instead, the bear fell backwards. Maybe it was instinct, to go back to the water. Maybe it was half-dead after I shot it. Or maybe it just chose to dive in the water because it thought it would be the safest place.

The currents quickly just took it under. The bear just as easily could have thrust forward at us, though, and that was what I was expecting. I thought the polar bear would have a last-gasp charge in it. We would much rather have retrieved it.

This polar bear may have weighed fifteen hundred pounds once, but it was half-crazy with hunger. Generally, polar bears gorge themselves until they store up a lot of fat and they live off the fat for a long time. This one was lean, too lean. It didn't have enough fat stored to protect itself against the long winter. It got hungry and was attracted by the smell of the whale.

Whenever you're butchering a whale on the ice, in the spring or the fall, you have to be ready for polar bears to surface. They smell dead whales and they come. This bear was seen in the distance by others and we were told it was headed our way, so it wasn't a shock when it found us. We heard there was a polar bear sighting, so we kept an eye out for this rascal. We were lucky enough to have a little advance warning.

Even so that bear almost sneaked up on us. You have to react quickly when you see the bear. When the bear came up on us I only had time to think where I was going to shoot it and what to do if it jumped. The whole incident took less than five minutes. It was a very long five minutes, though.

Polar bears roam the far north year-round. In summer they don't come into the town of Barrow. You can see the edge of the permanent ice pack in the distance on the horizon and the bears stay way out there most of the time. They have dens. They mate in the spring and have their offspring. They do snoop around any whale bones late at night near Point Barrow when people are sleeping, but as a rule they don't come around people who are out and about doing things during the summer.

I know most people in the world only see polar bears in the zoo, but they are a fact of life where I live. They're not in cages, either.

Polar bears don't usually want confrontations with man, but they're not easily scared, either. In the wintertime and springtime, polar bears might walk right into downtown Barrow. It happens regularly. Or maybe irregularly, you might say, since you can never predict when it will occur. You must be alert.

It's just a fact of daily life living in the Arctic that a polar bear might stroll your way when you're doing your shopping or driving along the street. I guess in some parts of Africa people who live in villages might be alarmed when lions or other beasts come to town. Same with us and polar bears.

We're not just talking about the outskirts of the community, either. In wintertime, polar bears come into town several times. They might be walking down the street between the high school and city hall, just like another curious pedestrian or tourist. Only they're looking for food. Not long ago one polar bear walked right up to the Browerville section of town and on into Barrow to the upper lagoon. That's just a few hundred yards from the center of town.

If a person sees a polar bear coming he is supposed to get on the VHF radio and report it. The alert goes out that a polar bear has been sighted nearby. The police or North Slope Borough public safety department get involved and the North Slope Borough Wildlife Management department brings in special cracker shells.

Polar bears are a protected species that have not been hunted by the general public since 1972, but Eskimos are allowed to kill them if necessary. Almost always it is considered in defense of life and property if a polar bear is walking through town where your kids are running around playing. We don't routinely hunt them. I think we'd rather leave them alone. But you are allowed to defend yourself.

Polar bear meat can be a tasty game meat, but stay away from the liver. The liver can have deadly poison. It has certain proteins that can kill you. If you are going to eat polar bear meat you've got to really cook it a long time.

A lot of times polar bears can be scared away from Barrow, but other times nothing will frighten them off. If they do come all the way into town, we almost always have to shoot them. Intense hunger rules their thoughts and they're not going away on their own. We usually have no choice. Generally, when they actually come into the city, they are losing their judgment. They are only interested in being fed. They might be mad from hunger, and that makes them very stubborn.

One time I was parked in my truck, just sitting there out on the beach overlooking the water, when four polar bears came right up close to me. There was a really big one, the mother, who was probably an eight-footer, two small cubs, and one older cub.

There was a polar bear alert in effect already and I had my rifle handy. I was ready to shoot. I was on polar bear patrol, working to make sure the bears didn't do anybody any harm, to make sure they went away. It was kind of a crazy scene. Many people drove their cars out from town along the beach road to look for the bears. As if they had never seen a polar bear before.

One of the polar bears came right close to my truck. If I'd pulled forward I would have had a polar bear passenger. Instead, I backed up a few feet and then I blasted the horn. The noise startled the bear. It ran a few feet, but then stopped and started towards me. I still think that a lot of the time the bears are more scared of us than we are of them, but this one was not easily distracted.

The biggest danger from that family of bears would come from the mother. Momma bear would be protective of her young and if she sensed a threat from an unsuspecting person, watch out. I don't think those bears were as insane with hunger as some other individual bears who wander into town. They were just walking out on the shore road. Maybe they were sightseers just like the people who drove out to look at them.

I think I see at least one polar bear every year in some circumstance, in town or on the ice. Barrow might be the only town in America which has signs posted that say, "Watch out for Polar Bears." I think when visitors see those signs their eyes get really big.

When you are hunting for whales and leave the carcasses on the outskirts of town and bring all the whale meat into town, there is going to be a smell that lingers and that attracts polar bears. It's just like when you're walking past a restaurant and you smell the inviting aroma of a hot meal. That's what the bears are thinking about, so it makes perfect sense they want to follow their noses to where the food is.

We put up warning signs right after the whaling season. Just a reminder to people that polar bears might be in the vicinity. You might see those signs in places downtown, but a lot of them will be closer to the butchering sites. The bears will hone in on the area if they think they smell a free meal.

When people in Barrow hear about a polar bear alert on the radio, it's something they take seriously. They don't blow it off. They believe it, even if they do drive their vehicles out on the road to watch sometimes. But they understand polar bears can be dangerous.

You put out an alert telling everyone to stay away except the police and polar bear patrols and they come out anyway. Especially tourists, who sometimes act like idiots. They want to see the wildlife. Some of them don't know any better. You tell them to stay away and it's like you are telling them to come. It's just a fascination with polar bears, even if it's not behaving too sensibly. People come to Barrow expecting to see polar bears so they want to see them when they hear they are around.

Local people remember things that have happened before, though, when there has been a polar bear encounter.

A few years ago, a man in a nearby village was badly mauled by a polar bear. It was dark, and he was just walking between buildings, close to the door of his house, and he died. He was only trying to get home with his wife, who was pregnant, when the polar bear came up on them. He distracted the bear so she could get away and he ended up sacrificing himself for his wife and kid. People know polar bears will eat a man. They know all too well that if they are out hunting seals on the ice that a polar bear might be tracking them, too.

Just because polar bears are big doesn't mean they are slow. They are not only very powerful since they can snap your bones with their jaw, or knock you dead with a single swipe of a paw, but they are very quick. If you have ever seen a leopard leap, polar bears are just as fast.

Polar bears have an interesting lifestyle. They mostly live on the ice, but they are very much at home in the water. They are excellent swimmers. They can swim twenty miles in a day easily. They run fast and they swim fast. Swimming is all they do in the summer, swim, swim, swim. All the way to Siberia and back to Alaska. The ocean is their swimming pool.

Once, I was out duck hunting with another guy and we saw a polar bear in the distance. He raised his rifle and took a shot at it. This time, I guess, the noise frightened it away. It just took off running. It was something to see. This bear was jumping from one pressure ridge to the other. Graceful, smooth. Pressure ridges are bumps on the ice and they are usually hard to cross. I had never seen anything move so fast through pressure ridges. And there were open leads in the water. If I had been running through there, I would surely have fallen through the cracks into the water. But this polar bear made its way through fast. Even on thin ice. Somehow, heavy polar bears are able to stay on top of the ice and not break through. I don't know how they do it.

Watching a bear move across very thin ice is educational. They have really adapted to the environment. I think that somehow they are able to distribute their weight. They spread out their front paws flat and start to crawl, pushing themselves along with their hind legs. It's not something humans know how to do yet, but a polar bear knows. On the same piece of ice, a person who weighs much less would fall through the thin ice, but a bear can equalize its weight. Even when polar bears are hunting, they use their front paws like skids to creep up. They use their rear ones to push forward and they sneak right up on their prey. You never know where they came from. Very stealthy animals.

In the dark or the dimness, or even in the sunlight sometimes, you might drive by a bear and never notice. That's a polar bear's protective coloration in the environment. They are very well camouflaged. Out on the ice you might drive a snowmachine right past one and never know it was there unless it moved.

One time one of my uncles was driving a snowmachine down a trail near town and a polar bear was walking right down the trail in the opposite direction. My uncle almost collided with it.

The polar bear just ran off. I think it was startled by the nearness and the roar of the machine. My uncle was plenty scared, too. Polar bears are pretty formidable beasts. You don't want to tangle with them. Just leave them alone. Stay out of their way. He was lucky.

This is polar bear country. The bears are used to this land and move easily in it. The elements don't seem to bother them much. They are built for the harshness of the land and the winter. Most of the time they are not noticeable to us. Most of the time I think they're trying to avoid us, too.

Chapter 22

Even though winter is settling in on us and it's already dark around the clock, one of my favorite times of the year is still the holiday season. I really enjoy Thanksgiving time and Christmas time in Barrow.

During Thanksgiving, we often are still sharing a whale caught in the spring. And Christmas time we are involved in playing the Native sports. So they are both great times of celebration and they help lighten the mood for everyone at a time when it's cold and dark out.

Those whales are so huge that not only do we share pieces of them in the spring, there is enough left over to share again. About a week before Thanksgiving we use cut-up muktuk and load them into boxes and pass them out to people.

During the Thanksgiving period everybody in the community gathers in all of the churches and the whaling captains stop by and drop off loads. The church leaders divide up the meat among all of their churchgoers. The bounty from the hunts of geese and ducks and caribou get shared at this time as well.

The same big whale that is hunted in the spring just lasts and lasts. Not only for Thanksgiving, but for Christmas feasts, too. That is a tradition for all the whaling communities of the entire North Slope Borough. It's another whaling festival, Thanksgiving right on through Christmas. Christmas is the last day that the spring whale is shared by everyone.

Then the Christmas Games begin. The competition begins the day after Christmas and runs right up until New Year's. A whole week. I always tell my friends from the World Eskimo-Indian Olympics that they must come to see what our games are like and some of them who have competed so well over the years have come to visit. Nicole Johnston from Nome and Greg Nothstine from Anchorage have made a trip to Barrow to see how we do the games.

I have always taken an interest in the competition at WEIO to spot rising talent like Nicole and Greg, Carol Pickett and Asta Keller, and Brian and Sheila Randazzo. They are a generation younger than me, in their late twenties or early thirties, but their careers overlapped with mine and I watched them and wanted to teach them.

At WEIO, I feel I am like a scout, always looking for talent that can be developed and just as importantly looking for people who not only have talent, but look like they can be examples for even younger people coming along. We always need teachers and I look for athletes to teach.

I encouraged all of my younger friends, but I also took the time to talk to them and let them know what they were getting into. By that I mean I took them aside and made sure they knew the traditions. When they showed interest in what I was saying about the history of the culture I stuck with them. I won't be around forever at the games, so we always need new people to come along and take our places who can ensure the future of the games.

It's not just physical talent that I'm looking for at the games. Attitude is a big part. Heart. I'm not impressed with how good you are. I'm a picky person.

I sensed that I could plant a seed with these particular young people and it would grow. A lot of times those special types of athletes make themselves known to me. They come to me for advice. They know I was a good athlete, so they might ask me questions. They might make the first move and I use that to introduce myself. We chat and I tell them how they can improve. But all the time I am looking and watching to see if they are listening and showing interest in more than just improving their high kick or whatever.

During this time I am trying to break through the walls and barrier between a current athlete and an athlete who may be a lot older. Then I can start submerging them in the knowledge of the culture, just the way my elders taught me.

Still, I must say that if I never went back to the World Eskimo-Indian Olympics I would still have concerns about the future. I am comfortable with Brian and Sheila and their efforts to preserve the culture, but as I have said before, I get concerned when others try to change the rules of the games. So I do worry.

I set very high standards. I have a responsibility to the elders, so my standards have to be above and beyond reproach. I do not take this responsibility lightly. What needs to be, needs to be. Things must be preserved and people must be told why the games must be preserved the way they are. That's one reason why I like my WEIO friends to come to Barrow. It's one way to get them to understand where I'm coming from.

Going to WEIO is one of the greatest Native social gathering events of the year in Alaska, as well as a sports competition. My parents, Robert and Martha, always go, too. They are part of a Barrow dance group. I have never been part of the dance team, but I love watching it. My favorite thing is the stories behind the dances. The dancers perform at festivals, at the Christmas Games, at WEIO, and sometimes they get invited to other places, too.

So many stories. The dances tell about hunting trips, happy times and sad times, about everyday life and welcoming in the New Year. I wish that everyone watching knew what the subject of the dance was.

After the Thanksgiving and Christmas festivals, it's really the heart of winter in Barrow and it's a quiet time. There's no hunting or whaling then. That's when I take every opportunity I get to go to Anchorage or Fairbanks. I probably go to Anchorage five or six times a year and Fairbanks twice.

One reason I am attracted to Anchorage is shopping. Really. There are a lot of big stores with a big selection of things, unlike Barrow. Another reason is mountains and sun. We only have tundra in Barrow. It's flat and wide open. I really like mountains, though. When I look at mountains I'm always awestruck by the beauty and the majesty. I have always been very interested in all aspects of nature, but to tell you the truth, I would like to drive right up to the mountains because it is a humbling experience.

Now, about those trees we don't have up north. That's another of my fascinations. Out of this little seed comes one great big tree and that makes you think. A tree is something small and it starts growing and branches out. And it brings not only shade, but happiness, joy. People start noticing the fruit of it. A tree of life. It stands there absorbing all this moisture from the ground and grows. We never think about it being alive. It endures the winter, storms, but every year it comes back strong. There's an awful lot to like about trees.

I must admit, though Barrow is my home and always has been, I have been tempted by the idea of moving to the big city of Anchorage. Once, when I had a job at Prudhoe Bay I was going out with a girl who was from Anchorage and we were getting pretty serious. We actually went house hunting there. This was a long time ago during the oil field boom times. But when we broke up, that was the end of that. I stuck to Barrow.

It might seem that I would be giving up too much of my lifestyle if I moved to Anchorage, but I didn't look at it that way. I would just have to come back to

Barrow to hunt. I would never give up the hunting or whaling. Living in Anchorage would only be in my retirement from my job driving heavy equipment.

I wouldn't look at it as a real retirement, though. If I moved to Anchorage I would have a purpose. I once heard a person say that sometimes you can do more for your country if you leave your country. Maybe I could do more for Barrow, for Inupiat Eskimos, if I left Barrow. I would promote. Maybe I could do more for a Native corporation or my people if I was in the big city, near the hub of the population.

Naturally, I would stay involved with Native Youth Olympics and World Eskimo-Indian Olympics. Sometimes I think if I had my way I would like to move WEIO from Fairbanks. I don't think it would get lost or overshadowed in a smaller city. I think it might become more popular, that it might attract more fans or tourists. There might be more visibility for the games and there might even be more financial support from big corporations which are located in Barrow or Nome.

WEIO has been held in Fairbanks for its whole existence, more than thirty-five years, and it has become a summer tradition there. I admit that it might sound funny for someone who believes so strongly in tradition to talk about changing something like that, but I do believe it might be better for funding the event.

I am sure that Barrow would be a very popular site for WEIO among the competitors, but I know it would not be among the dancers. Fairbanks is easier to get to for the dance groups who fly in from the villages and it would be a longer trip and more expensive for them to go to Barrow. We couldn't please everybody. I'm not even sure my parents would be excited. I don't think a change would be going against our heritage or our ancestors. It would be a worthwhile test for a year to see.

Barrow is very big culturally and with 4,100 people it is a big enough place. One attraction for athletes is that there would be more tradition linked to the games. Others might argue that it is too far away and WEIO could get hidden away behind all the other activities. I don't think so. I think it would be very interesting to see the place that is the origin of a lot of the games.

I know it's a controversial idea, but as a vice-president of WEIO and a former president, I feel it's my responsibility to bring it up. Other board members agree and still others disagree. I'm ready to have a discussion that is controversial if I think it will improve things.

People might be surprised. I feel that if we are barely getting by in Fairbanks and a corporation wants to finance the event and they make a condition of financing it to move it out of Fairbanks, that would be okay. Let's give it a try. Go with it.

Chapter 23

Storytelling is a big part of the Inupiat Eskimo culture. It's huge. It's what keeps our traditions alive and it's what keeps our culture moving. It helps keep our lifestyle lively and colorful.

I am a storyteller myself sometimes. Of course, I tell the stories of how the Native Games originated. But I also tell stories that I have heard from my grandparents. It's just passing on information that I have been given by my elders.

I thought everyone had heard the story about the ten-legged polar bear. Well, anyway, my uncle told me that years ago and I've already mentioned that tale. When people get together they also tell stories about their hunting events and near-death experiences. These stories carry a message that whatever we do we must do it carefully. We live in an unforgiving place where the elements are harsh and it is important to be reminded of that. Telling stories is sometimes the best way to get warnings across instead of just lecturing.

Through stories you can learn what is unsafe to do, that if you don't heed warnings, you can be seriously hurt. You can learn how to go out and hunt a certain animal, even to learn what time of year to hunt.

We also like to pass on funny stories. Here's one I heard a year or two ago:

There was a man who was going hunting on a snowmachine. He was a few miles outside of the village and he saw some caribou in the hill country. Some of these hunters who are very good can just jump right off their snowmachine while it is still rolling, get their rifles out, aim and shoot within moments.

Well, this hunter said he was going along chasing the caribou and he jumped off his snowmachine just like that, really quickly, and shot one. Good shot. The caribou went down.

The hunter wanted to go over to examine the dead caribou and when he turned back to his snowmachine he was shocked to see that the machine was still going! The throttle was stuck and the machine was just going in circles. Every time the hunter got close to it the machine was just a little bit too fast for him and he couldn't quite catch up. He kept stumbling in the deep snow. He would run after it, and just when it seemed he might get it, he would lose his footing. Around and around it went. Finally, the hunter gave up and stood there watching it.

Then another idea came to him. He thought, "Ah, it will eventually run out of gas."

So the hunter went off to butcher the caribou and wait for his snowmachine to run out of gas. He worked over the caribou and that kept him busy for a while. When he looked up, though, he noticed someone on top of the hill in the distance with binoculars. He was just praying it wasn't one of his friends.

The hunter started to wonder how long this person had been up there watching him. Did this person see everything happen? The snowmachine going in circles, him stumbling in the snow? The hunter thought this person must have really been laughing at him. Sure enough, the person then came down to help him and he had been watching for a little while. They sat down and they had a good laugh.

True story.

Other kinds of stories involve shamans and stories of strange lights and strange sights. Ghosts. This is a land where over time a lot of people have died from diseases like tuberculosis, smallpox and other sicknesses, so there really were mysterious things to be frightened of. At times those illnesses almost wiped out the Eskimos around here. You hear stories that are kind of scary from past storytellers who tried to explain the mysteries.

I have experienced seeing a strange motion. Well, not really seeing it. I think it was a ghost. We were kids and we were walking along the coast with my grandmother. We were walking along and saw something come right over us. But we looked back and there was nothing there. Was that a ghost? We were in flat country, it was wide open and we could not see anything around us. We were near the cliffs miles out of town, but they were too far away for anybody to be hiding there.

My grandmother said to us, "Don't bother it! Leave it alone! Don't mind it!"

My uncle was with us and when we turned right around he shot aimlessly with his pistol. Then we ran all the way home. As we were running home, one of my cousins started going, "Oww, oww, oww." Like somebody was hitting him. He stumbled and fell, but we couldn't see anything. We went in our tent at hunting camp and we were so scared. My grandmother just said for everybody to go to sleep and forget about the whole thing.

Later, were in bed in our tent and our rifles were resting against the wall of the tent. And all of a sudden we saw the walls moving from side to side with nobody touching them. My uncle ran outside, but there was nobody out there. Again my grandma told us to go to sleep. That was her advice for us in those situations. She said, "They never bother elders or old people."

I have no idea what it was on the coast or in the tent.

We have heard stories about little people in the Arctic, though. Legend has it these little people are good hunters and can carry a bull caribou and that they are truly out there. I don't really know who the little people are, but so many people have said that they exist that it is not up to me to say that they don't. They are manifestations of something, maybe something that happened a long time ago.

There is a large wooden boat that sits in the lagoon near downtown Barrow, just a few hundred yards walk from the government buildings and the stores. Some people think that it is haunted, but I don't know about that. I think some people like to keep others away from the boat with stories so they can go in there and drink. Other than that the boat is abandoned. It's said that people are seen moving around in the boat and that people hear noises.

Of course, my grandfather who I listened to when I was young, was a big storyteller. I think most of the stories we are told as young people have some message or moral to them. Real things that are incorporated into stories that are supposed to impart some bit of wisdom or advice to us about living our way of life or surviving. Sometimes the message of a story can be as simple as telling us to always carry a long stick with you when you go on the ice. Or, to never go out alone.

Now that I think of it, there were a lot of stories about the little people. Some people said that in the old days they used to commune together at first, but then they would separate and live among us.

Another kind of story about something being haunted that I remember is one where we kids were told there was somebody outside the entry way of the house and that if we opened the door we might startle the little man.

Our relatives told us that we might see the little people out there. I opened the door because I wanted to see them, but I never saw one.

Chapter 24

The airlines that fly passengers to Barrow and other cities of the far north in Alaska give away certificates which congratulate people on crossing the Arctic Circle.

We Inupiat Eskimos live above the Arctic Circle. We're here all the time. To the tourists who come to visit us, though, that's a pretty special thing to do once. But I don't think I ever mentioned it to anyone, just in that way. I don't say I live above the Arctic Circle. I just say I live in Barrow. Or, I live as far north as you can go in the United States.

People pause when they hear me say that, but I don't think they realize what they're hearing. People's sense of geography is not very good. They don't even realize where Alaska is, let alone Barrow or the Arctic Circle. For most people this Arctic Circle business means nothing. Until I show them on the map. It's just talk until then. Then when they see for themselves on the map, they can visualize it. Then they truly realize Barrow is at the top of the world.

It's funny, to most people, if I say I come from Barrow, they just think it is another big city outside of Anchorage somewhere, never realizing it is as far north as they can go. It's a fact, though. My home is the top of the world.

Once you point it out, they get interested. And once you point it out, they start to become interested in visiting Barrow. We get thousands of tourists. It seems unbelievable. If I show them Barrow is at the top of the world, then they go, "Oooh, what's up there? Is it frozen all the time? Does the snow and ice ever melt there? What do you do? Do you live in an igloo?"

These questions start rolling in. "What's the weather like? What about the winter? Is it dark?" Some people even say, "How can you live there?" Or "Too cold for me." They didn't think the world could get that cold.

I have heard some very dumb questions from tourists over the years, though it's been a long time since I heard a really good one. "Are you an Indian?" That's one I got a lot. "Do you guys still eat raw meat?" Or "How can you live up there?"

One of the best questions ever was, "Does it snow in Barrow?" I don't know what that person was thinking.

And I've been asked how come there are so many Asian people in Barrow. There are some Asian people in Barrow, but I think they were looking at the shape of our eyes and couldn't tell the difference between Eskimos and Asians. The polite answer would be to tell them that we are all related.

One time I told some people that it can snow in July, because it does. They thought I was kidding. But it is a fact. Just a fact. Can't dispute this fact. It's reality.

People really don't know much about Barrow unless they make an effort to educate themselves by reading a lot. And they don't usually do that unless they are going to make a trip to Barrow. Some people think we're all Indians. Many, many people don't even know Inupiats exist. In some cases where they think they do know about us, it's a cartoon image.

I honestly have no idea why people think Eskimos kiss by rubbing noses. We don't. We never have. I have never built an igloo myself in my life, except for the times fooling around as a kid. No kind of snow dwelling. No snow houses. Not once in my life, except play time. Canadian Eskimos have built igloos. We just use some of the snow for insulation around the tents we put up. We create snow walls to block the wind. That's all. But no, a thousand times no, we do not build igloos for our homes.

The old images carry on because of Hollywood directors and especially old movies. They gave Eskimos names that made no sense, that aren't Eskimo names. Names that sound more Japanese than anything. Like Timko. That was a name in one movie. Or Oogala, which sounds much more like something from the Hawaiian Islands. It's a made-up word. The movie directors didn't know one thing about the Inupiat language.

There is one movie in particular that I think of very negatively. "The Giant Snow Bear." It's an old movie, but the actors are still alive. In fact, one of them attends my church regularly. Unfortunately, people who don't know any better will believe what they see in the movies. Which is crazy, if you think about it. People watch James Bond movies and they don't think the stuff that happens in those movies is real. Why do they think that movies that have Eskimos in them are the truth? But that's the way of the world, I guess. Movies do have power to shape public views.

To me it's somewhat dangerous that that happens because it seems it works the same way for the government and the International Whaling Commission. They say the whales are getting to be extinct and they don't want us to hunt them anymore. At the same time, we are out on the water here seeing thousands and thousands of whales swimming by. For those government officials to be sitting in their ivory tower somewhere in a big city and saying we are hunting whales to extinction and that we are to blame for the decline of the whales, it is just ludicrous. We laugh at them. We see plenty of whales with our own eyes. And they make their fancy scientific determinations without ever coming here. Same thing as believing in igloos and rubbing noses.

If people think they know something about Eskimos, they should come to Barrow to find out for themselves.

Most of the people who visit Barrow come in the summertime. Let's face it, the average person would rather go to the beach in the winter than be in Barrow. Only a diehard person would dare come to Barrow in the dark of winter. And it is the dark of winter. It is more of an accurate picture of what Barrow is like to come in the winter, though. There are some people who drop by in the winter out of curiosity. Mostly Japanese tourists. They come to see the northern lights and see for themselves the actual climate.

But most tourists come in the summer.

The most famous thing that's ever happened in Barrow was the 1935 plane crash that killed Wiley Post and Will Rogers. They were two very famous men in their time. Post was one of the best pilots in the world. And Rogers was famous for writing and talking and telling jokes. He was very popular. When they crashed their plane in August of that year, it made news all over the world. People still talk about it today and the fact that it occurred in Barrow is one reason why people still come to visit today.

Even the Inupiat of Barrow still talk about it because the incident involved one of our elders, Clair Okpeaha. He is the one Wiley Post and Will Rogers talked to when they first landed the plane at Point Barrow. They were lost and they were looking to make it to town in the fog. They were on their way to Barrow to visit with Charles Brower, the old whaler. Clair gave them directions, they took off, and they crashed right there in the water.

That part of the lagoon is very shallow. I think I know exactly what happened. They were taking off and I believe they hit a sandbar and just flipped upside down. When I go out there in my boat I am traveling along and sometimes I hit one. They probably hit with the plane's skis. When I'm in my boat, I'm going along the water and all of sudden it's a total stop. If you hit a sandbar, it throws everything in the boat forward. It's not too bad if that happens with a small boat, but with a plane that's taking off, it's not too good. Once, I broke the front window on the boat. If you hit a sandbar you come to a dead stop. You don't sail over it. I think when Wiley Post and Will Rogers came to a dead stop the impact is what whipped them right over and they crashed.

Clair Okpeaha was nearby and he tried to save them. Then he ran all the way back to town to alert people about what happened. After a while they put up a memorial there for Wiley Post and Will Rogers. Then, because it was too far away, they put up another one right in town, not far from the airport. It's just down the street from my house. The tourists all stop there and take pictures.

It's pretty amazing that so many tourists still have an interest in something that happened sixty years ago, but it's also understandable. They were pretty famous people. I just wish the tour guides would talk a little bit more about the role of Clair Okpeaha. They don't talk about the runner who went for help. We named a building after him in town, the fire station. They put up a Wiley Post-Will Rogers monument and we put up a building for Clair.

The original memorial was a stone steeple, but some people defaced it. They broke off pieces. They wanted parts for a souvenir. A few years ago a new monument was put up. It has engravings of Post's and Rogers' faces and stories about their exploits. I guess it makes sense that they put up a new one because all these tourists come to see something about them and before they couldn't see it twelve miles away. They were probably very disappointed.

I'm sure that some of the tourists come just because they heard this is where Wiley Post and Will Rogers died. That puts us on the map. For others, I'm sure it's incidental. We get a lot of tourists who come just to see for themselves a place where the sun is out twenty-four hours a day in the summer and to go to the farthest north place you can go in America.

Chapter 25

It took more than fifty years after the deaths of Wiley Post and Will Rogers for another huge event in Barrow to catch the attention of the world. That was the famous operation to rescue the three stranded gray whales in the ice of the Arctic Ocean.

And what a strange event that was. Between October 7 and 27 of 1988, the eyes of the whole world were on Barrow. Millions of dollars were spent to rescue three whales who forgot to swim south for the winter. They usually follow the bowheads south for breathing holes. These whales got themselves in a fix and if they hadn't been seen just offshore, they would have been trapped under the ice and drowned without anyone knowing.

We figure that this happens every winter, or almost every winter. It's part of survival of the fittest in the north. No one ever knows how many whales die this way. Only this one time, because the whales got trapped under the ice right next to land, they were seen, their whereabouts were reported, and the media went crazy.

The gray whales weighed about 50,000 pounds apiece each. Their snouts and skin were scraped and raw from banging against the ice, trying to reach holes in the ice sheet so they could surface and breathe. People thousands of miles away who never saw whales before started worrying about them.

Ordinarily, the whales would be gone from our waters by early October. They swim south, past Canada's Yukon Territory, Seattle and Puget Sound, and California and all the way to Mexico where they spend the winter before coming back to the Barrow area. When they first were spotted, some Barrow whalers were interested in harvesting them. Remember, it's normal for us to hunt for whales, though we go after bowhead whales, not gray whales. But when everyone else got interested in them, people around here thought it would be better to try to help the whales escape than to hunt them.

This was another case where a lot of people didn't even know that Barrow existed until they heard about the whales. The whales were featured on TV on the national news and all of a sudden everyone cared, reporters were coming from all over the United States and other countries. Everyone wanted to save the whales and everyone wanted to see the whales.

We sure did make a lot of money off the media. Oh yeah. When reporters came to town with their cameras and their notebooks they all had to go out on the ice a few miles to see the whales themselves. It happens all the time that whales get stuck if they leave late to swim south. It was just the first time the media noticed it. These whales were lucky. Or they had a good public relations agent.

It sure did surprise me how big this event got. Hundreds of people came to little old Barrow to help the whales, to see the whales, to take pictures of the whales. It got kind of crazy because there was no room for everybody. Barrow is a small place and in 1988 it had even fewer hotel rooms and restaurants than it does now. It got really overcrowded. The military was involved, the best Eskimo hunters who normally would be trying to harvest the whales were helping to try to rescue them. At one time there were a hundred Eskimos out on the ice cutting holes so the whales could move from blowhole to blowhole and be shown the way to open leads so they could get away.

I helped a little bit with the chainsaws making breathing holes in the ice. I was just pushing ice, keeping an eye on the equipment. Not doing too much.

At first, I thought it would all just pass over and that all the excitement would quiet down in a few days or a week or so. Everybody would leave us alone and the whales would die. But it got bigger and bigger, went on and on. Everyone short of President Reagan came to town, it seemed. And he was on the phone!

I kept thinking how gray whales follow the bowhead whales when they leave and if they get left behind when everyone else goes, they die. Happens all the time, no big thing. The whole matter got blown way out of proportion, but I'm glad it did because the Eskimos of Barrow were the ones who benefited. We got the best end of it.

It was just a silly, silly thing. It was magnified by the news media and the save-the-whales people, the animal rights activists. They even named the whales, Sikhu, Poutu and the baby was called Bone. I'm sure the animal rights people were overjoyed. We saved a whole whale! We did good!

I spent most of my time watching this whole circus from a distance. To me the most impressive thing was the Russian icebreaker they brought in to help. That big ship just plowed through the ice and really opened it up for the whales to get away. Our boys couldn't do it, so they did it. That was embarrassing.

As usual, I was going to work most days operating heavy equipment. I got overtime money out of working on smoothing the road so the reporters could get out to Point Barrow. We took a warmup shack out there, tractors, chainsaws, gasoline, a couple of loaders, and we made the road drivable for the reporters. I just did my job, and except for a little work on the ice I didn't get too involved with the whales. The interviewers were just there for sensationalism, anyway.

A lot of the Eskimos made a lot of money off the reporters. Some of my cousins drove reporters the four or five miles out to the whales by snowmachine and they charged them outrageous fees. The going rate was more than a hundred dollars each way, but at times they could charge much more. I'm sure they even got $1,500 for a trip. I know that sounds unbelievable, but the reporters were desperate. Fifteen hundred dollars per person on a snowmachine. People paid that. Those Outside reporters and camera crews had to be desperate. They got sent all the way to Barrow so they had to see some whales no matter how much it cost. I guess people act funny and lose all common sense when they are desperate.

On the job, while we worked on the roads, we were just joking about it all. We laughed about it all. "Can you believe these reporters?" we'd say. And we talked about how people were making a ton of money. We started trying to come up with ideas how we could make some money and make plans if it ever happened again.

One idea we had was to bring a sled out on the ice with a covering and open up a snack bar out there. It would have been like Gold Rush days in Nome. We could charge outrageous prices for a dozen eggs or a hot cup of coffee. We'd milk 'em. Stuff like that. We were just kidding around.

I'm still waiting for whales to get trapped again and have the media come back to take pictures so we can have another chance to get rich. Chances are, though, it's never going to happen again. Whales will get trapped again, but nobody will notice, or say anything.

Still, lots of people know where Barrow is now who didn't before, which is not a bad thing. Trapped whales won't ever get so much attention again. Not like that.

Whales do get trapped under the ice and die. That's part of nature. We shouldn't try to change nature. For all we know a dozen more whales have been caught in the same circumstances since then. I don't think anyone's covering it up, but

I'm sure it's happened farther away from shore where men didn't see it. This was not a new occurrence for us when it happened in 1988.

This type of thing happens pretty fast. All it takes is for the ice sheet to close up so there is no place for the whales to breathe. They rub their skin raw on the ice trying to break through and the next thing you know they get hypothermic and they freeze. If there is a cold snap in the fall, that's it. I'm sure whales have drowned since then and we didn't see them. Positive. I have no doubt it must have happened again in the years since. Without the whole world noticing.

One of the great mysteries is what happened to the gray whales once they were freed, after all that effort, all that time and money that was spent to get them on their way. The baby whale disappeared even before they got away. I'm sure it died then. No one knows what happened to the other whales. People who were watching like to think the whales got away and lived happily ever after, but they were never seen again, so we don't know. They had a long way to go in their weakened condition. They were in danger of not getting enough food and running out of energy. When they left here, after their ordeal, they were sick. They were in poor shape. I don't know if any of them survived. They might have all died.

The animal rights activists and other people want to believe it all worked out okay, and even though they followed them for a while as they started swimming south they lost them. Honestly, I think they probably all died. With the kind of injuries those whales had and the kind of exposure they got, I don't think a whale can live very long. When they broke free of the ice they still had to get past ice floes, killer whales and great white sharks to reach the warm water of their breeding grounds. They were battered and bleeding, so the odds were against it.

The entire scene was way too peculiar for us. Inupiat Eskimos hunt whales to survive and here we were rescuing whales. Too many people around the world cared too much about the whales. It made me think that their priorities were all wrong. Their priorities should have been for the children in the United States who were starving, not with whales. To me it was a waste of a lot of money when they could have been feeding a lot of kids in our own country who need help. So much money went for the whales, so many millions of dollars, when it could have been spent on food for people. The priority of our government and other nations was just all focused on the wrong issues.

If there was one good thing that occurred, the whale rescue showed there can be cooperation. There was cooperation between other countries and the United States and Eskimos and other people. So perhaps it served a larger purpose. I could never understand how it was really worth it, though. I remember one Eskimo from Barrow made a joke to someone who he thought might be an animal rights activist. He said, "Well, I'm here, but I brought my knife and fork with me!" It turned out the guy was just one of the reporters. I thought that was pretty funny.

To tell you the truth, I was on that guy's side. The whales could have been lunch. Hah, hah. I was prepared to eat them. I was willing. They have pretty good tasting meat, those gray whales. Get me my knife and fork. Bring it on!

People in town don't really talk about the whale rescue anymore and only a few tourists bring it up from what I hear. Mostly, it's forgotten given how much excitement there was. I know one guy even wrote a book about the whole thing. Pretty amazing, but since it had so much attention, I could see how that would happen.

The whale rescue was one of the most famous things that ever happened in Barrow and it certainly put us on the international map for a while, but it is long over for most of us. History. Dead issue. Dead whales probably, too. The feast that could have been.

Chapter 26

All those reporters who came to Barrow for the whale rescue were lucky it happened at the beginning of winter. They never would have stayed around for as long as three weeks if they had come in the summer. The mosquitoes would have driven them away.

We have polar bears and bowhead whales, but the most fearsome creature in the north land is the mosquito. One mosquito is nothing, but even two are a threat. You can capture one and kill it, but if two are around you already know you've got a problem. Because while you are killing the first one, the second one is sucking you dry.

I think mosquitoes work in teams. "You go in now and I'll suck this guy's blood." They do a tag team on you. Just like those professional wrestlers.

Of course, you never see just two mosquitoes. In the Barrow area we get millions and millions of mosquitoes. Sometimes they come along in a wave so thick that they make the sky go dark.

I have been told a story — and I believe it to be true because I was told it by some of my uncles — about how one time they were walking from their cabin inland and there was this odd-looking black cloud in the sky coming towards them.

One of my uncles said he told his family to put their faces to the ground and not to look up. Their orders were to hide inside their parkas and stay there until the mosquitoes passed. Isn't that something? Picture a whole family huddled on the ground for protection inside their thick coats, scared to look up in the air. I have heard stories about clouds like that which have killed a person. They just suck all the blood out of them.

There are more than two hundred different kinds of birds which migrate to Barrow in the summer, and a lot of bird watchers come to town to see them. That's not something I can identify with, it's not an activity I can appreciate. It seems kind of silly to travel thousands of miles to just look at the birds, but they do it. The funny thing is that there is a joke here that the Alaska state bird is a mosquito. Now that I believe. I don't think tourists come to watch the mosquitoes, though.

Generally speaking, there isn't as much of a mosquito problem in the city of Barrow itself. Just in the area. And especially inland where we go to hunting camp. Barrow is usually safe because we get cool breezes from the ocean. The wind makes all the difference. It keeps them away. But if you go four or five miles out of town, whew boy. South or west, they are manhunters. They will eat you alive.

The millions of mosquitoes are one reason why so many caribou die off. The mosquitoes get them and the caribou get sick and weak. They are always running, constantly running from the bugs. Sometimes when you kill a caribou for food, there's hardly any fat left on them. They burn it all up running in circles from the mosquitoes. I think sometimes life gets so unbearable for them they run to the ocean and jump in just to get a brief respite from the mosquitoes.

For someone who has never experienced this kind of mosquito swarm it is very hard to believe. One summer not too long ago I was on my way to my boat and I was wearing just a windbreaker as an outer garment. Big mistake. I even had the hood from my jacket pulled over my head. I also had bathed myself in mosquito repellent from top to bottom. I literally put it all over my face and hands. Every part of exposed skin was covered. But then I started sweating and it washed off the protection.

I had just stepped off the small plane about sixty miles from Barrow and started walking on the way to fish camp when I was surrounded by a swarm of mosquitoes. I soon started noticing bumps on my skin. It was awful. Every time I breathed in, I sucked in a few bugs. I started spitting and there were bugs in my saliva. It was nasty.

Through my hood I could actually hear thousands and thousands of mosquitoes hitting against the windbreaker. It sounded like raindrops hitting my body, only it wasn't raining. Actually, it was raining mosquitoes. It seemed like sand was blowing against me, they were that thick. All over me. It was maddening. I could hear punctures on my hood. Thousands and thousands of mosquitoes trying to get at my blood.

Here I was, already dipped in repellent, but they still came. They got all around my mouth and the area around my lips was covered in bugs. I know I swallowed a bunch of them that day just walking to the cabin. My cousins were with me and they didn't put too much repellent on them and they got it really bad, even worse than me.

The absolute worst part of it all was that the cabin wasn't safe either. It was so hot in there and when we opened the door the mosquitoes followed me inside. We fired up a mosquito repellent coil and finally chased some of them out of there. But it was torture, just torture. I remember starting a generator so we could get a fan going. Some of the mosquitoes were smart. They stayed on the outside of the generator because they liked the feel of the vibration. There were so many mosquitoes gathered there, just huge gobs of them, that it seemed like a mass of moving jelly.

The mosquitoes that weren't so smart got caught up in the generator and there was a big pile of dead mosquitoes. After a little while, so many mosquitoes got wound up in the generator that it was just shot. The mosquitoes inside the generator just killed everything, just stalled my generator. I had to clean out the filters before I could start it up again.

And you know what? There are more and more mosquitoes each year. I am convinced that there were more mosquitoes in 1998 than there were in 1990. I don't know who would take the census count to prove it, but that's what I believe.

I'm pretty sure the mosquitoes are getting more and more aggressive each year, too. They never used to go with us way out on the ice, but now they do. And in the summertime, forget it. When you are way out there in a boat, when the ice is melted, they stay right with you, for twenty or thirty miles. I swear it's the same mosquito who follows you for twenty miles, right from shore, until he finally gets to suck your blood. They are persistent. They just come right at you relentlessly.

Sometimes I think it would be a lot easier to wrestle a polar bear than trying to contend with our mosquitoes. It makes you wonder. A dozen Barrow mosquitoes or one polar bear. Hmmm. An even match.

Chapter 27

Mosquitoes have been with us my whole life, but when I was growing up in Barrow there were hardly any cars and trucks around. That's something that's really different now.

When I was a kid when the supply barge came to town it was the highlight of the whole year. To see this big ship come in from Seattle and land near your beach was something else.

And the captain of the ship would come in with all these goodies, hard rock candies and stuff. We knew that our stores would be filled again and we'd have fresh, well not fresh, but real fruits and vegetables. Fish, candy, a lot of things the rest of the world had just by walking down to the corner store was all brought in for us.

We were really isolated in those days and you couldn't get shipments of goods with the same ease that we get things by plane now. The ship came in only once a summer when the Arctic Ocean was thawed and open. It was really wild. When the barge came in with all these things there would be tremendous anticipation in town. Everyone would work to unload the barge. The whole town. The routine of daily life changed as soon as the boat arrived.

Some people ordered fancy things for themselves that were delivered on the barge, but we weren't ever that rich. One of the things that always came on the barge that I got were boxes of Sailor Boy crackers. I grew up on those things, thick, unsalted crackers which stayed fresh. They would bring in boxes of them by the thousands. Thousands of boxes. They would last the rest of the year. We wouldn't run low until the next ship came in. The arrival of the boat was really something to look forward to. It represented contact with the outside world, too, at a time when we didn't have nearly so many visitors as we do these days.

Now, for the most part, every day something comes in to Barrow. By airplane, or even by a barge from Prudhoe Bay. The big supply barges still come in during the summer, but they mostly only haul large equipment and fuel nowadays. It's not as much of an event as it used to be for us.

There are no shipments by truck or car since there are no roads which lead out of Barrow. But there are plenty of vehicles inside the city. There were very few cars in Barrow when I was a young man. The cars came along much later with oil money. No one could afford cars before. We were just subsistence people then, eating off the land. When we started earning money, everybody started buying cars, snowmachines, four-wheeler ATVs, trucks, boats, anything they wanted. They had the money then.

The first method of transportation my family had when I was a kid was a dog team. Then a snowmachine was the only way we could get around. Now I drive a Chevrolet Suburban. Big vehicle. I bought it used in Anchorage and I drove it up the haul road — the Dalton Highway — they use for trucks to bring things to the Prudhoe Bay oil fields. And then I had my car shipped to Barrow from Prudhoe Bay.

Actually, at first I just drove the three-hundred-and-sixty-five miles from Anchorage to Fairbanks and left the car there for a few months until it was time for the barge to come to Barrow in the summer. I picked it up and I drove it right onto the barge. Then I flew home and a couple of days later the barge got to Barrow and my car was home. Obviously, it still takes some planning to get a vehicle to Barrow. And the shipping charges are very expensive. Just to ship the car directly from Anchorage to Barrow would have cost me $4,000, so it made sense to drive it as far north as I could.

That's a lot of postage, isn't it? As it was, it still cost me $1,500 in charges from Prudhoe Bay. You hear a lot about dealer destination charges everywhere when they get a car shipped from the factory to the showroom to sell, but I think this would be the all-time record. There aren't any automobile factories near Barrow, that's for sure.

Just to give you an idea how far away we are from everything, in 1991, when I bought my twenty-foot aluminum boat in Fairbanks it took three weeks to get it to Barrow by plane.

There's no railroad, there's no highway, so the only way to get big things from

Fairbanks to Barrow is by air. That's the only way. Well, you could haul something by snowmachine in the winter, I suppose. Or, in the middle of winter, you can drive a truck on a trail between Barrow and Prudhoe Bay and then drive on down to Anchorage. That would pretty much be a serious adventure drive.

We have plenty of troubles with cars in Barrow in the winter. They were built for use in the lower forty-eight, not for starting every day when the weather is at thirty degrees below zero. It's often too cold for a vehicle to start at all. You've really got to winterize them. Most of the cars we have were not built with Barrow in mind. Maybe for Hawaii. Can you believe that I have air conditioning in my car? And can you believe that I have actually used it in Barrow? Really. On a seventy-two-degree day. Otherwise I'll use the air conditioning a couple of days out of the year to see if it still works.

To be honest, we're usually a lot more concerned with whether or not the heat works than the air conditioning. You have to do a lot of preparations to winterize a car properly for use in Barrow.

You've got to put heating plugs on both sides of the truck just to keep the circulation going. You need an oil pan heater, a transmission pad. Then you put a battery jacket on the battery. Then you put a certain kind of oil inside your engine. You have to make sure your gas lines don't freeze and use a certain kind of grease for all of your fittings, for all of your moving parts. You have to make sure your heater is in perfect working condition. There are so many things you have to do and even then the car still doesn't always start. You just never know.

All you need to prevent your car from starting is a good cold snap. You're in trouble right away if you forget to plug it into an electric heater at night. You'll find yourself with a frozen engine. Anything below minus-forty and you are probably not going to start that thing no matter what. Or a minus-eighty wind-chill factor, forget it. You walk to work, or take the snowmachine.

The car should start at minus-twenty, no problem. But when you have a few days of minus-forty it gets touch and go whether it will start or not. And even sometimes at minus-twenty-five or thirty. Plug-ins only work to about minus-thirty.

Snowmachines are more reliable than a car. We will use them instead a lot of the time in the extreme part of winter. Most machinery does not like cold weather, but snowmachines usually do great. Not all of them. Some of the cheaper ones are hard to start. Depends on what kind of snowmachine you buy. Your top-of-the-line snowmachines don't even always start in our cold weather. And we are led to believe they build them pretty tough. Mostly, they will start if you take care of them.

There should be no cold that's too cold for a good snowmachine. Let's face it, they are not building snowmachines for the Hawaii market like they do for cars. They'd better start.

Chapter 28

Barrow was always the friendliest of towns when I was growing up. We didn't have television and we didn't have many visitors, so everybody socialized by going over to each other's houses.

Now it's grown quite a bit larger and not everybody knows each other. It's just too big. Most families stay by themselves a lot now. They rent videos and stay home. It still sort of has a small-town atmosphere and most people recognize each other, but with more than four thousand people everyone isn't as close as they used to be. You can't know everybody anymore.

Being in Barrow my whole life I certainly know a lot of people. And I have a lot of relatives in town. I couldn't even count how many. I still keep finding out how I am related to them. The number keeps growing. Maybe I'm related to almost all the Eskimos there. My father was one of seven children and my mother was one of eight children. I have so many cousins. And I have nieces and nephews I'm still finding out about.

I also have a lot of relatives in villages all over the North Slope on both sides of the family. They're spread out all over. I am a single man and it seems like every time I meet a pretty Eskimo girl and get to know her I find out later that we're related. I guess that happened four or five times in my lifetime. I would meet the girl at village get-togethers, or in some other way outside of Barrow, and we would be flirting and the next thing you know we would discover we were related. We always turn out to be cousins and we're not allowed to marry our cousins.

When I was younger, the families were closer and you never had to lock your door at night. That still continues to some extent, but you don't know all the people anymore, so you can't trust them. There are too many other people in Barrow. Not too long ago someone stole a fur parka from a home. They just walked in the door of a house because it wasn't locked. In another case, an old man cooked his supper and then went to church. While he was in church, somebody just walked in his house and ate all his food. The outside world has moved in on us surprisingly, and with it, crime.

Barrow was a more innocent place when I was a youngster. It was more of a village than a city. We were more innocent people. We were a gentle people, happy, satisfied, debt-free, living off the land. Just happy.

Things changed, though. We had no other choice but to try to master both worlds. You either follow or get out of the way. Lead, follow, or step aside. And so our elders said, "Let's lead."

Over the years, archeologists have come to Barrow and found artifacts and more recently tourists have come to Barrow to buy things to take home. I don't collect very many things about our culture. I'm not a collector, or a saver, I guess. I save most of my medals from the Native Youth Olympics and World Eskimo-Indian Olympics. But I give some of them away, too. I don't save much of anything. Just the memories.

I do like to see tourists buy things so they can remember Barrow. Baleen baskets or carvings. Once when a tourist bought a baleen basket I told him that the product he was looking at came with a lot of sacrifice of time and energy and I told him where the material came from. It took a whaling captain one season and a lot of money and time to go out and capture a whale so he could feed the whole community and out of all that work finally it comes down to this. After a long season of storing the food, he finally gets down to stripping the baleen and makes it into a baleen basket.

On top of that, going after the ivory at the base of this baleen basket is something else. Same thing, going after a walrus. A lot of effort. Tourists don't always realize all that goes into it. So the price set on a baleen basket is very cheap compared to what must be done to get the raw materials to make such a thing for you, Mr. Tourist. The tourists are getting a bargain.

No tourist buys something unless it captures his imagination. They see something they like, they buy it. They spend a lot of money to come to a place like Barrow by airplane that's so far north and what they buy reminds them of the place they visited where the sun doesn't set and of the people of a different race.

When they return to their big cities and look at this carving they bought, perhaps they think of the people of this land. They tell stories to other people about what they experienced when they went there. So one day other people might come, or they might want to come back again.

I think it is a good thing. When people come here it teaches them that this place is so unique and bewildering.

Many years ago, the archeologists and scientists came to dig in Barrow and they took away the bones of many people. They did this all over the north. Now they are starting to return the things they took.

We are learning fast. Things that weren't of value to us back then, seventy-five years ago, are important now because we are losing sight of who we are. I think because we are in danger of losing sight of our heritage and our culture that we are starting to worry. Our elders are dying off left and right and taking with them vast stores of knowledge that has not been passed on to our young. Things we should know about. A lot of times they die off too fast and all we have left is the artifacts.

Back when diggers were taking bones and artifacts that were in our backyards, they used to exploit us. They made money off of them selling them to museums. No one really protested at first. Later, nobody was listening. Now there is increased sensitivity. Across the street from the Arctic Pizza restaurant in Barrow, there is a sign that tells people not to touch anything in the field. That sign would not have existed years ago.

There used to be a disrespect of the Inupiat Eskimo way of life and our existence, selling things to museums. No one would try to take the bones now. That's progress. Now that we are more financially secure we have taken it upon ourselves to get educated. Along with this education comes political power. Our people who have been educated felt they were being taken advantage of. Our younger generation felt we were being robbed of our rightful heritage.

The scientists have stopped trying to take our bones away and now the government is even returning some of what they took before so those remains can be given a proper burial. The younger generation showed them it was wrong.

A few years ago in Barrow they uncovered the bodies of what was called "the frozen family" in the ice, where they had been for hundreds of years. If that had happened during the 1920s, they would have taken them away and been kept in some museum, probably frozen so everyone could see them. It would have been a tremendous insult. Instead, they are buried in Barrow. What was learned was precisely what our elders tell us about the harshness. That family was crushed by the ice that trapped them.

I had two beautiful nieces, eighteen and nineteen, who were digging for artifacts along the cliffs on the edge of town and there was hanging ice. It collapsed and crushed them, killed them.

The "frozen family" was crushed by sea ice moving in. People don't understand what a powerful force the ice is. Once, it came close to crushing our old house when we lived along the shore. This was a one-story house, about twenty-five feet by forty feet. It would have reduced it to splinters. Giant, solid blocks of ice piled up maybe two or three stories high moved into town. The ice just piled up bigger than any building in Barrow. It got to within a hundred yards of our house. We were evacuated. The National Guard was called up. I remember watching the ice move really fast. Every time you turned your head it had piled up even more. It was an amazing and scary thing to see.

I had seen a movie once where a railroad train just piled up so fast, all the cars jack-knifed and folded up and crashed. The train stood right up and fell over and the ice acted the same way. Only it was more powerful than that. It came close to ruining many buildings. I think we were lucky that no house was touched. The ice would have torn our house up, leveled it to the ground, turned it into driftwood.

We had plenty of respect for the ocean, but this gave us even more respect.

More recently, another individual turned up in the ice and the scientists said his body was from the 1200s. Almost eight hundred years ago. And to think, they had no rifles or ammunition or snowmachines. Just bows and arrows and no western influence. No boats. Life sure must have been hard for them.

They were living off the land the same way as we were. Sometimes I wonder what it would be like if I lived at that time with those people, or if I met them. I believe I would have something to talk to them about. Our interests might be very much the same, hunting for whales, hunting for caribou.

Knowing that there was a land bridge from Siberia tells us a lot, that we had a kinship with other people from far away, with Natives from all over the world. I think of those people as brothers. People from Siberia, Japan, Greenland, Canada, Iceland.

I am sure all the people of the north had the same philosophy of dealing with the toughness of the elements.

In Barrow, we were always taught not to waste anything. We picked up lots of driftwood and scraps of metal. Our houses were made in part from shipwrecked ships and whatever we could find. The masts of sailboats stood up in town to be lookout towers for polar bears. Nothing was ever wasted. If I had an aluminum can, it would be made into something. It might be flattened out and put on the wall for extra insulation from the cold. We split open cans and made them into something useful, a tool, or a sled runner. Or maybe the metal would be a patch for something. It could end up on a boat. If you were wasteful, you were not a good provider.

The same rule applied to the food we ate. You were never allowed to say, "I don't like this." You were expected to eat it, whatever it was. You couldn't blurt out that you didn't like it.

No doubt all of the people of the north who were in cold climates and who were isolated from big cities lived pretty much the same way.

Since the Cold War ended between the United States and the old Soviet Union, there have been a lot of links established between Alaska and Siberia. I have not made a trip to Siberia, but I know people who have. They drove snowmachines to Siberia. And others went from Little Diomede Island to Big Diomede Island. From the United States to Russia, it's only two miles or so there. The languages are not all that different. The dialects are a little off center with ours, but not altogether different. They felt an immediate connection to those people. The food they were eating was the same.

I hope eventually that Siberia sends a team of competitors to the World Eskimo-Indian Olympics. They have sent some people to the Arctic Winter Games to participate. They were part of the entertainment, though. What they did seemed like circus acts. What I want to see was the games they learned.

One thing we are always asked about our language is how many words for snow and ice Inupiat Eskimos have. I don't know, but I saw that the government or the North Slope Borough has a list of seventy-six words for ice and a list just as long for snow. Really, it's just different forms of ice and snow.

In my mind, there are just a few words for ice and snow. "Sigu" is ice. "Apbun" is snow. All of the others are just related to ice and snow. Snowflake, newly formed ice. They are varieties of meaning for ice and snow.

We have so many words that are about ice and snow because those are the elements we are most concerned about in Barrow. Winter always meant getting serious, though less so now. In the old days we lived more day to day and prepared for the harshness every day.

When I was a boy we didn't have running water. I remember going out to the ocean and chopping up ice with an ice pick. We brought home the blocks of ice by sled. We had to melt it. It was hard work. We had enough ice for just a few days. And then we had to do it again. If we were lucky we had chunks of ice that had drifted and we could pick them up.

There was no shortage of work to be done when we were kids. You can bet that we had words for ice that we gathered, but maybe you don't want to know about them.

The word "Inupiat" describing us means "The real people." To me, it means we were the first people. I believe not only Inupiats, but Indians have their tribes named as the first people. Others say the same thing. We were all here before Columbus came. Columbus said he discovered America, but we were already here. The Eskimos and Indians both are the real people. We spread from the north as far south as Florida. We all migrated out of the same area, across the land bridge, across North America. We just chose to stop here in Barrow. We were not claiming this was our land, we were just choosing to live and die in this place. Some Natives were pushed aside by white men and pushed into corners of the country.

I do think calling ourselves "the real people" indicates a pride in who we are. But being part Irish, that makes me think. Look how far those ancestors of mine came just to make a living. They got stranded in Barrow and were thinking of their folks back home even as they started a new life in Alaska. It's like having two different worlds bound together in me.

Chapter 29

When I go to work I usually wear blue jeans or sweatpants and a windbreaker over a T-shirt. I wear baseball caps a lot. The same as many people around the United States. But I also have traditional Eskimo clothing that I wear often. Many times just for special occasions.

I wear mukluks, the handmade foot gear that is sewn from caribou skins and one of my most prized possessions is a fur-ruffed parka made for me by my mother, Martha. It's blue velveteen with the trimmings that are her trademark. I try not to wear that too often because I want it to last and I don't want to get it dirty.

My mom has her own designs and it's her signature. She made it by hand. It's like the coat of many colors for Joseph in the Bible. When you see an Inupiat parka you can tell who made it by the markings. It's just art, her own art, but it's very special to me. Nobody else does it. It's her markings from her heart to her son. It is difficult to say exactly what it is like because it has personal meaning. It's mostly sentimental.

When I was younger more things were made by hand than they are now. I had a really thick parka made out of caribou skins by my mom. I was never cold when I wore that. And my feet were always warm in my mukluks. I'd wear those mukluks until I got holes in them. I'd wear those things out. I had a couple of pairs. One was from caribou hides and the other was from bearded seal. One of those pairs even had some polar bear skin in it.

From the time I was a little toddler until I outgrew them, that's how I dressed. It wasn't until at least middle school that I wore any clothing that had any western influence. My mother spent her whole life sewing. She made clothes for all the kids.

As we grew up, we grew out of our clothes and she made new clothes. It was a lot of work. But she was considered one of the best seamstresses in all of Barrow. She also did special work for others, fancy stuff. Although I don't ask her for anything, once in a while she surprises me with something like a beautiful jacket.

My mother's eyes aren't as good as they were, though, so she doesn't sew nearly as much now. That's one reason why I save my favorite blue parka for special times. I know she might not be able to make me another one ever again. It means too much to me to get it all torn up. I take it out for whaling festivals, the Christmas Games, big gatherings, family events.

Like I said, it has sentimental meaning for me. And as I get older I think about those things more. I think I have gotten more spiritual as I got older, too. Not like when I was a wild high school kid.

I have come to the conclusion that my physical strength comes from inner strength and that inner strength comes from God.

My mother likes to tell a story about me and one of my brothers, when I was about fourteen years old. There was a truck that got stuck out on the beach and the owner tried to free it up, but couldn't. He went off to get a shovel and some help and while he was gone my brother and I moved the truck. We were strong enough. We just used mind over matter. We pushed it out. It was a combination of brute strength and knowing what to do. We just had to lift it up a little bit. It was using our heads as much as our arms.

I guess that adds to my reputation for being strong, but really, it's about using a combination of smarts and strength. You don't really think about those things then, or the fact that you are stronger than the average man. Until one day you notice that you did something that no one else could do.

In the Bible stories, Samson never really knew his own strength until someone told him. Then he realized his strength came from God. I think we all grow up like Samson, not knowing our own strength.

I have come to learn that my future is not determined by me. It is determined by the Creator who put me here. I feel that I need to reach out to young people and that's one reason I was put on earth.

When I think of someone I want to be like for the rest of my life it is Samuel

Simmonds, one of our elders who died not too long ago. He was a gentle, soft-spoken man who wanted dearly for his own people to understand what the Lord was saying to them. It wasn't really religion that he was preaching so much, but a way of life he was trying to get across to people, that we should all do things in Barrow that we were born to do. We could serve God and set an example. I admired him very much.

That is the life I aspire to lead and I want to show kids that way of life. Samuel Simmonds made carvings and through them he showed our people beautiful things. He could look at a piece of ivory and picture exactly what he wanted to say. It was his way of telling a story. The end product was a story. A hunter talking to a little boy, a student learning from a teacher.

He was also gentle. He never used harsh words. This man set a fine example. And when I spoke to him in Wainwright once he said I was doing good. He said we need more Inupiat ministers. He meant that literally, but I think he spoke more spiritually in general.

I was brought up Presbyterian. It may have been a white man who brought the religion to us, but the way I look at it, we all came from one race. We are all God's people. There were missionaries who tried to make us do everything their way, or else. And there was some bad feeling about that. I grew up that way with religion pushed into my face. I didn't know then that there were all kinds of people who pushed all kinds of religions down people's throats without respect for their cultures. Or really, without respect for anything.

The devil has no respect for human life. If I see those kind of people, I know they are not serving God. Jesus set an example. He didn't go to the big churches. He went to a park and to the sinner who needed to be saved and he ministered to them.

I think the missionaries who came to Bush Alaska had good intentions, but they just got overzealous about saving souls. I think they just went too far and saving souls became an obsession. Then they lost sight of God and his values. In doing that they weren't teaching the proper worship.

I was about thirty years old when I shifted the focus of my relationship with God. When I started reading scriptures I realized that was meant for me. It's been about fifteen years, but I am still learning a lot of things. If I had one wish for the Inupiat people, it would be that as one race we would go through the Pearly Gates of heaven. Man, that would be something.

To reach that point, though, some things would have to happen. We would have to have a change in attitude. We would have to start changing inside. We would need closer family relationships. We would need the holy spirit to deliver us.

I think these things could happen if everyone regained their focus and put their priorities in the right place. Perhaps there are things in this life that we could all still do in heaven. Maybe we would all enjoy going seal hunting together.

Seal hunting in heaven. That's what I'm wishing for, what I would desire. You never know. There is more beyond the skies than we know about.

Chapter 30

When I think about the future I mostly think how I want many things in my life to continue the way they have been. I want to keep whaling and hunting for bearded seal.

I love it when you hear on the citizen's band radio that there are ugruks out there to be caught. I like just getting in the boat and going out there to see for myself. And going around the big icebergs and trying to see the bottom of the icebergs. It's thrilling. And actually capturing a seal, that's the highlight.

One thing that makes me worry a little bit about the future is the weather. The climate is changing. Some of the currents seem to be changing. The water temperature seems to be rising. I can sense it and if you listen to the elders they will say that the water is warmer than it used to be.

We have been seeing this for about five years. You hear about the hole in the ozone in Antarctica and these kinds of things make you wonder about the north, too. Global warming. The elders know about this, too, and they talk about it.

This could mean that we are getting down to the age of destruction. There is so much pollution in this world. I know that the more people we have the more pollution there is. There's no turning back. I know that's not a very optimistic outlook, but I'm afraid it is the truth.

I know people are trying their best to clean up what others have created, but they are not doing well. In fact, I see destruction happening faster than they are cleaning up. There are men in this world who would gladly blow up other countries without even thinking.

A couple of years ago in Barrow the ocean did not freeze up until December. That's not normal. We had open water until early in that month. We delayed going out for fall whale hunting because we were all just amazed. The Chukchi Sea froze and the Beaufort Sea didn't. The Beaufort Sea stayed open. That means there's some kind of new activity or pattern going on underneath the surface. To me that would mean global warming is a lot closer than we thought.

I believe that some parts of the world's oceans are now so polluted that the whales will get sick. And not only the whales, but the whole chain of life. When one part is extinct, the whole chain goes with them. When we try to change one thing, or get rid of one animal, we upset the entire balance and wreck the whole thing. Like when people try to eliminate wolves in order to allow the caribou herds to grow so they can hunt them. They never think about what they're messing with.

Since I was always large for my size and for most of my life have had the nickname Big Bob, I never thought about what my life would have been like if I had been a small person. It never crossed my mind and when someone asked me about that it was something that surprised me. If I was smaller, for sure, my name wouldn't have been Big Bob. Maybe it would have been Little Bob.

And I wonder if I ever would have been involved in the World Eskimo-Indian Olympics, which has been such a big part of my life. I always did the strength events. I don't think I would have been in WEIO if I had been a small man. It seems like small Eskimos, who are really wiry, are good hunters. Maybe I would have tried some other events at WEIO, but maybe I would have been too busy being a hunter.

Of course I was always a big eater and that helped me become Big Bob. Maybe Little Bob would have had a big appetite, too. I am blessed because I am the world's largest Eskimo and I wouldn't want to change that.

When people ask me how I would like to be remembered, I find it difficult to say. I don't want to sound boastful. I think of Samuel Simmonds, though, and I think of the leadership he showed. I would like to be remembered as someone like that old man who worked to set a good example for the people who came after him.

I aspire to lead a good life and I hope that people will understand that. In your lifetime, you always wish you could correct all the mistakes you made. It would be satisfying to know you had corrected all those wrongs, but you could never do that. When I was younger I messed up in school, I drank too much, I had a temper, I got in fights and I made people mad at me. I don't do those things anymore. But there are always going to be mistakes in there that I remember that can't be fixed by me. Only God can fix them.

I just do the best I can do and I hope that when young people look at me now they see someone who is living a good life.

And I have a good life in Barrow. When the sun is out and the temperature goes up, Barrow can be a great place. You explore those icebergs and hunt the seals and you say to yourself, "What a life!" You just enjoy being out there on the water. I actually blurt out loud, "What a life!" I just appreciate being there.

One thing that makes it so nice is our air. I think we have the cleanest air in the country. I have been to other places and all you smell are exhaust fumes. It's just not crisp enough to be fresh air. In Barrow when you go out of town, you can actually smell the tundra. The sweetness of the grass growing and all the ice which has melted.

I enjoy it if we're in the boat on the water and we run into a herd of walrus and hear them singing. They make their natural noises in harmony. "Oop, oop, oop." Deep sounds. They move around and you hear it again. "Oop, oop oop." And there are thousands of them out there. You may hear them before you see them and think you are surrounded. You hear the perfect harmony.

It's a strange feeling. You are in the midst of this eerie sound, and enjoying it, but at the same time you never know if one huge walrus will come right out of the water and turn you over. So at the same time you could be in danger. Or you don't know if in the midst of this peaceful situation a big iceberg will head up the current and just ruin your day. Things change very fast. That's all just part of life in the north. You expect the unexpected. And you learn to accept it, or at least, live with it.

The ice will be with you most of the year, well into what is considered summer in other places. But even in June in Barrow you can look out on the sea ice and nothing will be moving. If the sun's out, though, as you look towards the horizon, you can see the beauty of this place. Yes, it's a harsh land, but we are blessed by what we have.

That's why the Eskimos who live in Barrow on the Arctic Ocean are the Frozen Chosen. It sounds strange, but that's us. The Frozen Chosen.